Overindulged Children:

A Parent's Guide to Mentoring

James A. Fogarty, Ed.D.
Licensed Clinical Psychologist
Certified School Psychologist

 Liberty Publishing Group
Egg Harbor • Frederick • Raleigh

Publisher's Cataloging-in-Publication Data

Fogarty, James A..
Overindulged Children: A parent's guide to mentoring./ James A. Fogarty.
p. cm.

ISBN 1-893095-21-5

1. Parenting   2. Interpersonal communication
I. Title

Library of Congress Control Number: 2003111719

10 9 8 7 6 5 4 3 2 1

"All children need three sets of skills before they can become adults. They need to know when to be dependent so they can heal from hurts, how to be kind so they can have quality relationships, and they need the stamina of self-reliance so they can stand on their own two feet. Indulged children learn to be over-dependent, and nothing else."

(Jim Fogarty)

Dedication

I dedicate this book to my Dad and my Irish uncles – the greatest mentors in the world. Each is filled with personality and dons a great smile:

- Adrian Fogarty – My dad and my all-purpose mentor.
- Myron Fogarty – The horse lover, who I spent many Saturdays with. He taught me to mentor children.
- Frank Fogarty – The mechanic who can fix anything and is outliving everyone. He taught me to mentor with humor.
- Hank Fogarty– The uncle with the greatest smile. He taught me to mentor with a smile.
- Lester Fogarty – The greatest storyteller. He taught me to mentor with metaphor.
- Emmett Fogarty – The runt of the litter, I enjoyed working with. He was a great mentor for hard and persistent work.
- Justin Fogarty– Died of tuberculosis before I was born.
- Ray Fogarty – Died during World War II in France.
- Justin and Ray taught me there is a limit to our mentoring and our impact.

Acknowledgements:

Family is the greatest concept ever created. Millions of families work throughout each day to love, talk, strive, survive, and bond. Families come in many forms and fashions. I would like to thank the families that have allowed me to enter their lives. I have learned from each family and I appreciate the education.

She organizes, helps everyone, volunteers, sells classic antiques, perpetually smiles and gets me to do projects I never imagined I could do. She is my wife, Cyndy. Because of her I have been on three-story scaffolds, built additions, built furniture, jumped off a cliff, installed a tin ceiling, written books, and lectured nationally. She shows me a picture of a piece of furniture, smiles and says, "You can do that!" Our favorite songs are "Hooked on a Feeling" – the Ooga Cuga version – and "Your Wildest Dreams." Married for 28 years—and it has been a wild dream to be hooked on this feeling!

The best feeling in the world is watching the birth of your children. The next best feeling is watching them become neat adults. They did it and I am very proud of Jason and Shawn.

As always, thank you God.

Contents

~ Introduction ~

Have you ever wondered why children seem more distant, even though this generation of parents has every parenting expert, parenting book, and helpful service available to them? Are you curious about why children have become bored, detached, and disillusioned, even though they have every entertainment available, and parents willing to amass 18% interest credit card debt to get it? Have you been sold on the idea that children are the greatest priority in your family, a greater priority than your marriage? Have you felt the pressure to buy the "right toy" for Christmas, with the belief that your child's Christmas would be ruined without it? Did you know that most homes have three or more televisions, with families detaching so each family member can watch their favorite programs? Overindulgence is creating distance, and distance is creating more dysfunctional families.

Today is a time of prosperity, but there are more children flunking classes, being truant, getting arrested, taking guns to school, dropping out of high school, and quitting jobs without notice than ever before. How have parents lost their influence with their children?

Well-intended parents have instilled within their children a false sense of self-esteem by overindulging them under the guise of creating "child-centered" families. The hope of many caring and well-intended parents is that their children would connect to their "child-centered" parenting with greater appreciation, love, and bonding. Instead, these children have more conduct problems, opposition, indifference, detachment, and feelings of entitlement, and are demanding more luxuries and freedoms from their parents than ever.

This book will reveal the indulgent beliefs which drive parents into overindulging their children. These indulgent beliefs push parents to offer a false love that gives children inflated and unrealistic views of themselves. You want to be close to your children. This book offers you the qualities of the mentoring parent, which will give you empowered hope. Of course, empowered hope is the first step toward positive change.

I once read a bumper sticker that said, "Now that I have given up all hope, I feel better." Nothing could be further from the truth! Hope is the wish for change. Taking action is the agent of change. This book will tell you what actions to take to become mentoring parents, so you can have a close relationship with your children.

What Is In This Book?

Chapter 1, The Types of Parents Who Overindulge, describes nine parenting styles that are indulgent. One excellent quality of most indulgent parents is that they dearly love their children. These parents have special and unique qualities, but problems arise when these special qualities are distorted. You will understand how and why caring parents distort their special qualities and become overindulgent.

In Chapter 2, The Distorted Beliefs of Indulgent Parents, you explore the indulgent beliefs that parents use. I also explain why these beliefs do not work.

Chapter 3, The Qualities of the Mentoring Parent, teaches you the solution for indulgent parenting. These qualities are not theories; they are practical and usable parenting beliefs and skills designed to replace overindulgent parenting. You will like these skills! They work!

Chapter 4, The Unsolved Mystery of Children's Misbehavior—Solved!, describes the motives behind children's misbehavior. You will learn the reasons for children's backtalk, nagging, whining, button pushing, scapegoating, lying and other unacceptable behaviors. It will become obvious to you how overindulgence makes your children's behavior worse! You also will build the skills to mentor your children away from these behavior problems.

In Chapter 5, The Toolbox for the Mentoring Parent, you will receive an array of parenting tools which, coupled with the personal qualities of the mentoring parent, will help you become the effective parent you want to be.

Let's get ready to change your basic beliefs about parenting and instill hope in your heart. Let's read!

~ CHAPTER 1 ~

The Types of Parents Who Overindulge

Overindulgence happens with wealthy families, middle-income families, and families that have little or no income at all. To clarify this, here are two definitions of overindulgence:

1. Parents with wealth or *false wealth* (credit cards) may give things to their children instead of mentoring their children. Without mentoring, children do not develop critical life skills, such as:
   a. Conscience development;
   b. Satisfying mutual relationship maintenance;
   c. Self-reliance.

2. If parents have no wealth, they may compensate by giving their children too much permission too soon, which often puts children in situations they are not prepared to handle. This also creates a secondary danger—it puts the children in the power seat of the family, without the information, skills, or maturity to handle it.

With these two definitions in mind, I would like to give you three examples. The first example is a wealthy family, the second example is a middle-income family, and the third example is a family with very little income.

The wealthy example:

In a wealthy suburb of Chicago, there is a beautiful high school surrounded by gorgeous and expensive homes. This sounds like a minor issue, but minor issues reflect major issues, because they usually reflect long-standing patterns.

A student of this school complained to his parents that he was having a trouble finding a parking place every morning, causing him to be late for school. Now, what would you tell your teen if he or she could not find a parking place for school? You would probably offer a simple solution to this simple problem. For example, you might suggest leaving earlier or commuting with a friend.

But his parents did not make these suggestions. Instead, they actually bought a second home across the street from the high school—just so their son could park his car in the driveway.

These parents are not teaching their son a basic life skill—how to manage a minor problem like getting to school on time. What will happen when he needs to make a serious adjustment to a major issue? For example, what if he witnesses the violent death of one of his parents in a car accident? This teen does not even have the skills to get to school on time. How would he ever adjust to a major life issue? He is not learning to manage even the simple problems of life.

The middle-income example:

When I go to Nashville for seminars, my whole family goes because we all play guitar. Nashville is guitar heaven and the center of guitar heaven is Gruhn's Guitar shop. As we were playing guitars, a mom was buying her 8-year-old son a $32,000 guitar. I knew this was a middle-income family because the mom told the salesman she had wiped out her retirement account to buy this guitar for her son. Because I am in Nashville, I thought this child might be a prodigy. I asked the mom, "Can we hear him play?" She said, "Oh, no. He just started taking lessons."

This child is not learning a life-sustaining skill: that as he progresses, everything will progress with him. Instead, he is learning that before he can progress, he needs the best—whether he can afford it or not.

The low-income example:

When I was a school psychologist, I worked for a very poor school district. This is another minor issue that became a major issue, because it reflected a pattern. A kindergarten student was enrolled in school, but was not showing up for class. It was a week into the school year, and he had not made a single appearance. I talked with the family by phone. They seemed like nice folks and very concerned for their child. However, two more weeks passed, and he was still not attending school.

With appropriate permission, the school social worker and I went for a home visit. The family lived in a mobile home, with a grandmother and great-grandmother living with them. As we all gathered in their living room to discuss the issue of their son's school attendance, this small boy was sitting on the floor, listening intently. During our discussion, he decided to demonstrate something for us.

He walked over to his dad, who was sitting in dad's favorite chair, and spryly said, "Dad, can I sit there?" His dad immediately popped up and let the boy take over the chair. The child sat there for five seconds. Then he went over to his mother and, with the same tone, said, "Mom, can I sit in your chair?" She immediately popped up out of her chair and let him have it. He sat there for five seconds, as he looked at the social worker and me and smiled. Then he went to his grandmother, who was obese and very unhealthy. In fact, she was on oxygen. He looked her straight in the eyes and said, "Grandma, can I sit in your chair?"

At this point, the social worker and I looked at each other with the same thought: "Is anyone going to stop this kid?" Believe it or not, Grandmother leaned against the coffee table, struggling to get up from the couch while pulling her oxygen, and let the child sit where she was sitting. He sat there for five seconds. Then he headed for his great-grandmother. Great-Grandmother, at 97 years old, was physically frail, but mentally sharp. She sat in a rocking-chair because it was easier for her to get up. The boy said to Great-Grandmother, "Can I sit in your chair?" She started rocking her chair, then propped herself up with her left hand and took a swing at him with her right hand. She did not hit him, and even if she had, she was too feeble to leave any marks. But at least she made her point!

Great-Grandmother was not raised to get up for a 5-year-old, but she was not in charge of the family. The boy's parents were—or were they? Who do you think was *really* in charge?

Imagine this child at 15 years old. You probably don't have to—I'm sure you've experienced children like this. They are creating problems in school, the community and the legal system.

A teacher with a very good work record went above and beyond when she assigned her high school students to write a term paper, which was a major portion of their grade. Being resourceful, she took the time to use the Internet, where there are resources teachers can use to determine if any students have plagiarized their term papers. This took extra effort and time on the part of this teacher. If they plagiarized, they did not really do the work—they cheated and lied. To her dismay, this teacher discovered that 75% of her students plagiarized! She appropriately failed the cheaters.

Because many of the students needed this credit to graduate, the parents sparked a revolution. Guess who lost her job? This teacher gave her students what they earned. She took the extra steps to be sure the students' work was legitimate, and she lost her job. The administration changed the students' grades and let them graduate. Professionals are actually losing their careers due to overindulgent families.

I am a parent and a psychologist, trained to be an advocate for "child-centered" families. On the surface, the phrase "child-centered" seems attractive and admirable. For many years in my practice as a psychologist, I promoted a "child-centered" approach to parenting. In fact, by using a "child-centered" approach, I believed I had the answers to every parenting problem. Then I had children! Befuddled, bewildered, and perplexed, I could not understand why these parenting principles I worshiped failed me.

Then I noticed something very important about families. Over the last 23 years of counseling hundreds of families, I have witnessed a transfer of family power from parents to children. This transfer of family power came under the guise of "child-centered" parenting, with well-intended parents blending a mix of advice from various parenting experts. Parents who deeply love their children have replaced mentoring their children with overindulgence. I believe many loving parents, driven by overindulgent parenting beliefs, are losing influence with their children. They are overindulging their children, not bonding with them.

Overindulgent parents have different styles of overindulging their children. Let's take a look at some of these styles and the impact they can have on children.

The Types of Overindulgent Parents

There are many different avenues for parents to overindulge their children. Most parents who overindulge their children have caring hearts and offer special qualities reflecting love for their children. Problems occur when parents distort these special qualities, and instead of giving children love and mentoring, they overindulge them.

Consider the following types of indulgent parents and their distorted thinking.

The "Giving" Parent

The "giving" parent is, as the name implies, a giver, which is a wonderful quality. Some parents, however, distort this special quality by giving too many material things. "Giving" parents buy their children\every brand-name toy and piece of clothing on the market. No expense is spared!

These children have bedrooms filled with televisions, computers, computer games, stereos, telephones, and more. Parents who give too much expect their children to reciprocate with appreciation and love. On the contrary, their children show little appreciation. Instead of love, these overindulged children feel resentment and entitlement.

Consider these examples:

During a counseling session with eight-year-old Ned, I asked him to describe his bedroom. Taking a deep breath, he said, "Well, I have a heated water bed and TV with a built-in VCR. It has a remote control and I am on cable with HBO and Cinemax. I have a private telephone line for my computer, and I'm on the Internet. I have Sega, Nintendo, Super Nintendo, and over 350 games. I have eight remote control cars and a remote control helicopter." Ned continued for ten more minutes. I checked my reaction, which was ENVY!

Elizabeth was a ten-year-old girl who refused to go to school unless she was wearing designer clothes! Her parents believed her desire to wear the best

clothes money could buy reflected her positive self-esteem.

When Brad graduated from eighth grade, his parents rented a limousine to drive Brad and his friends around town for several hours. Brad's parents said that this was the least they could do for him, as they were proud of their son. Brad was a bright child who was an underachiever, in the bottom 10% of his class—barely graduating.

Why would parents overindulge their children with expensive gifts? There are several common reasons.

The Distorted Thoughts of "Giving" Parents:

1. Some "giving" parents believe they are helping by giving their children what they never had when they were children. These parents are trying to fix their own childhood. In essence, these parents are overindulging themselves by overindulging their children.

   Even though most overindulgent parents strive for a loving relationship with their children, overindulged children rarely have a warm and loving relationship with their parents. When parents overindulge their children, they are not teaching their children to manage life. The children become over-dependent on their parents and often resent them. Instead of getting emotionally close, overindulgent children often separate from their parents—except when they want another toy, more money or a special activity.

This was the case with Ned, whose parents filled his room with expensive toys and goodies. Ned separated from his parents by isolating himself in his bedroom, which had become his cocoon. He rarely left his cocoon, refusing to participate in family activities. His parents' overindulgence of Ned created distance, instead of the love his parents were hoping for.

2. Some "giving" parents feel great competition with other parents who are also overindulging their children. To keep up, they excessively give to their children with a *keep up with the Jones'* parenting style. "Giving" is not restricted to families that have available cash. It also occurs in poor families. Many parents, without extra cash, create tremendous credit card debt (false wealth) for the sake of their children.

   Brad's parents (who gave Brad the limousine ride they could not afford) did not really want to reward Brad for graduating at the bottom 10% of his class. There were many rewards within their budget that they could have given Brad—rewards not involving exaggerated status symbols. They never told their family and friends the truth about Brad's underachievement. In essence, they were rejecting the truth of Brad's lack of achievement, because Brad was really a bright boy who chose to underachieve! Brad was wasting his brain! Instead of confronting the problem, his parents taught Brad to put up a false, face-saving mask to save him from embarrassment.

   Sometimes the truth is embarrassing—and it should be. For example, if you behave at work in a way that is embarrassing, that feeling of embarrassment inside of you teaches you lessons. When you attach good thinking to the uncomfortable emotion of embarrassment, you make a decision to never again behave that way at work. So, that uncomfortable emotion of embarrassment, coupled with good thinking, creates self-guidance. But Brad's parents erased his earned feelings of embarrassment by pretending he had been successful in school. His parents also erased Brad's chance to gain good self-guidance.

3. A few "giving" parents are prone to guilt. This often happens with divorced parents. "Giving" parents, with guilt, try to release their guilt through excessive giving. Even at a tender age, children with guilt-ridden, overindulgent parents learn to guide their parents toward guilt-reducing purchases.

   By using guilt trips, Elizabeth pressed her parents to believe her friends would ridicule her for not wearing designer clothes to school. Her parents believed her and felt guilty. By buying her designer clothes, they thought they were helping her create good self-esteem. But what Elizabeth was really learning was how to use guilt-ridden manipulation to get what she wanted.

Commentary

When overindulgent parents give to their children, they initially see joyful children, which is exactly what "giving" parents want. But "giving" parents have restricted parenting to one purpose—giving. The excessively "giving" parent is not teaching children to manage life, only to enjoy its indulgences. The children of "giving" parents do not become loving children. Instead, they harbor a deep sense of entitlement and resentment.

The "Reminder" Parent

"Reminder" parents have the beautiful quality of encouragement, constantly reminding and encouraging their children to behave. But one essential ingredient is missing with "reminder" parents: reinforcement. "Reminder" parents offer too many warnings to their children without backing up their warnings with discipline. They constantly repeat phrases such as, "If you don't stop that I'll..." or "If I told you once, I told you a thousand times...." Children, of "reminder" parents ignore their parents because they know their parents never discipline.

A lack of discipline offers children a lack of parenting, which forces children to create their own parenting. This allows children to 'take charge' of their family. "Reminder" parents create children who become powerful, but ineffective leaders of their families.

It is amazing how children actually want adults to 'take charge.' Here's a great example:

When I was a school psychologist, an inexperienced eighth-grade teacher lost control of her classroom. What a sight! Twenty-five eighth-graders out of control! The teacher asked me to meet with these children, without the teacher. I was forewarned that there were three children who were the ringleaders of the class. They were "in charge" of her classroom.

I gathered the class in a circle and they sat quietly as I asked my first question: "What do you kids want?" This question met with fifteen minutes of silence, which is a very long time with eighth-graders. Finally, one of the ringleaders pierced the silence when he said, "Structure, we want structure." I almost fell off my chair. I know children want adults to give them structure, but to hear one admit it in front of his friends was astounding.

The need for structure within these school children was strong. Their teacher would threaten them, but never disciplined them. The teacher offered no guidance on how to behave, so the children took total charge of the classroom. The same thing happens in many overindulgent families. For example:

A two-year-old boy was sitting with his parents in a restaurant. When his food came, his parents asked him, "Honey, who do you want to feed you? Mommy or Daddy?" The boy pointed at Daddy, and Mommy looked relieved. After dinner, his parents asked him, "Who do you want to clean you? Mommy or Daddy?" He pointed to Daddy, and Mommy looked relieved. When they were about to leave they asked him, "Who do you want to carry you? Mommy or Daddy?" He pointed at Mommy, and Daddy looked relieved. With these simple questions his parents are putting him in the power-seat of the family.

Although this young boy was obviously the decision-maker of the family, he was too young to know which parent was too tired or too stressed. That is a parent's job. His parents can better decide who should take care of him at any given moment. When power shifts from parents to children too early in life, it creates problems down the road. Bigger concerns arise as children become older and issues become more complex.

Duane, a fourteen-year-old boy, was getting aggressive. When he hit his brother, his parents reminded him to behave, but never disciplined him. He started hitting other children. In fact, he even enjoyed hitting his smaller friend, Jim. Duane's mother would always warn Duane

not to hurt Jim. When Duane ignored his mother and hit Jim, his mother warned Duane again, but never disciplined him. Duane was becoming a bully and his much smaller friend, Jim, grew tired of it.

One day Duane was riding his bicycle on the sidewalk. Jim was at the other end of the sidewalk calling Duane every nasty word he knew. Duane burned with anger and sped after Jim on his bike. Jim ran between two houses, through his grandmother's backyard, to a deck attached to the back of his grandmother's house. Jim ran under the deck and grabbed a rope. His cousin, Gary, who was hiding in a nearby shed, held the other end of the rope. Duane flew around the backyard at full speed, hit the rope and flipped off his bicycle, crashing into the gravel.

Duane's parents did not teach him that the "real world" will discipline his bad behavior, and the "real world" may not care about fairness and Duane's safety

Why would parents diminish their parenting role by only reminding their children to behave, without reinforcing it with discipline? There are several possible answers.

The Distorted Beliefs of "Reminder" Parents:

1. Some "reminder" parents enjoy giving the gift of encouragement to their children, but hesitate to take any disciplinary action. They want to be buddies with their children and fear discipline will hurt that friendly relationship. In my counseling sessions with "reminder" parents, they often say that determining when they should encourage, warn, and discipline children is confusing and scary.

On the other hand, I have many children tell me they know exactly how many warnings they will get before their parents give up in frustration. That is amazing! One child proved his theory by frustrating his mother in a counseling session. He quietly counted the number of reminders, until his mother finally screamed in frustration.

When parents offer no discipline, it leaves the children "in charge"—and they know they are "in charge." A great parenting technique for this problem is "one warning and a discipline." Always give only one warning. If the warning does not work, then discipline.

2. Other "reminder" parents lack assertiveness. They do not possess the skills of influence and action in many avenues of their life, including parenting. These "reminder" parents lack assertiveness with their spouses, bosses, in-laws, and others. They hope their children and others will be responsive to their words of encouragement to behave. Rarely do they take any assertive actions to enhance their assertiveness skills, including disciplining their children.

3. "If my children do not need to be disciplined, then I am a good parent." This is the belief of some "reminder" parents. They do not discipline their children, because they believe that if their children do not need discipline, they are good parents; conversely, if their children need discipline, they are bad parents. So their lack of discipline proves to "reminder" parents that they are good parents.

4. A few "reminder" parents just do not believe in discipline—period. They believe that discipline harms the natural development of children. If they impose the limits of discipline, their children will not develop into what nature intended them to be. I always give these

parents the assignment of reading the book *Lord of the Flies,* which illustrates how the conditions of life within society are closely related to the moral integrity of its individual members, and demonstrates what can happen with children who do not receive the proper discipline and moral instruction.

Commentary

When there is little guidance provided by their parents, children are set up to have problems. In his four short years, Jeffrey knew his mother was a "reminder" parent because he knew discipline would never happen. His mother constantly encouraged Jeffrey to behave, with Jeffrey ignoring her. He did what he pleased, seizing the powerful leadership role of his family. His mother never disciplined Jeffrey, which was unfortunate, because one of the goals of parenting is to prepare children for the real world.

When Jeffrey entered preschool, his teacher warned him once, and immediately disciplined Jeffrey when he failed to behave. Because discipline was new to him, Jeffrey had a tantrum. He did not know how to react to appropriate discipline. Jeffrey's parents had not prepared him for the real world, including the real experience of discipline at school.

The "Blinders" Parent

"Blinders" parents have the incredible quality of accurately recognizing the good in people. They correctly understand their children's good qualities and appropriately praise their children. This admirable quality becomes distorted, however, because "blinders" parents ignore flaws within their children. So, parents with "blinders" appropriately compliment their children for their positive attributes, but never give their children a correct appraisal of their flaws. As a result, they fail to teach their children how to improve their flaws.

When children do not receive an accurate appraisal of their flaws, they believe they are perfect. This results in an inflated self-esteem with a strong self-centered attitude. Because these overindulged children do not learn the valuable skills they need to manage their lives, they become over-dependent on their parents, never developing self-reliance or the skills necessary for mutual relationships.

Benny was a bright child who loved learning. His parents realized Benny was bright and they appropriately praised and encouraged him to learn. He was just starting his first day of kindergarten, and his parents had no doubt Benny would be successful. One of the first lessons his teacher discussed in kindergarten was the concept of sharing. Benny was not good at sharing, and his parents never corrected this flaw. As a result, Benny did not understand, nor did he like this idea of sharing. Benny decided that a classroom paintbrush was his paintbrush. When a classmate decided to use the same paintbrush, Benny felt justified in dumping paint all over his classmate's head.

Thelma's mother always praised Thelma's intelligence, and her praise was justified. Thelma was bright. In her first year of high school, she was at the top of her class. Thelma also had natural leadership qualities, exemplified by the way her friends looked up to her and followed her example. When a new girl started at Thelma's high school, Thelma had a choice. She could have helped the new student gain acceptance within her core group. Instead, Thelma constantly ridiculed this new student, and her friends followed suit.

Thelma had a strong need for status, which her parents did not correct. Because Thelma saw this new student as a threat to her status, she ridiculed her instead of helping her find acceptance. Thelma had a great potential for a beautiful skill (offering acceptance), but she had an uncorrected flaw (a need for status at the expense of others).

Both Thelma and Benny had incredible skills, but their parents never corrected their flaws. In both cases, the parents accurately praised their children's strengths, but failed to provide valuable feedback about their flaws.

Why would "blinders" parents accurately compliment their children, but avoid mentioning their children's real flaws?

The Distorted Beliefs of "Blinders" Parents:

1. Many "blinders" parents believe they will harm their children if they discipline them. They believe that to create good self-esteem in their children, their children should receive only positive messages. This complicates the lives

of overindulged children, as they eventually go to school, where both teachers and classmates give more realistic appraisals of positive attributes and flaws.

For example, many indulgent parents tell their children they are gifted, when they really are not. Many children are led to believe they will be the leaders of their class, but have uncorrected flaws that hurt their leadership abilities. "Blinders" parents believe they are helping their children by never mentioning these flaws. They miss many opportunities to help their children grow and develop. When the real world readily points out obvious flaws, these children become shocked. Instead of learning to cooperatively correct their flaws, they react with hostility, anger, and for a few—rage.

2. Some "blinders" parents do not see any flaws within their children. They have the distorted belief that flaws do not exist in their children, so there is nothing to correct. They believe that nature gave them a perfect child.

Thelma's mother believed Thelma was flawless. When she learned about Thelma's nasty behavior toward the new student, her mother immediately assumed the information was false. She refused to believe that her child would be so nasty, which prevented her from correcting her daughter's behavior.

3. Just as with the "reminder" parent, some "blinders" parents feel tremendous competition with other parents. To have an edge, they only see the good in their own children, while quickly spotting the bad in other children. When Thelma had her conflict with the new student, her mother believed there was a real problem: she insisted that this new student created the conflict. She rationalized with the school counselor, "Thelma was not in any conflicts before this new student arrived."

Blaming other children or teachers is not uncommon for "reminder" parents. They blame others so they can preserve a perfect image of their children.

4. Other "blinders" parents believe that admitting their children have flaws is an admission to being a bad parent. These "blinder" parents have their self-esteem wrapped around the image of their perfect children. If they accept their children's flaws, they are lowering their own self-esteem. To feel good about themselves, they must see their children as perfect.

5. When parents address their children's flaws, they commit to helping their children change their flaws. Some people dislike change, seeing it as something to avoid. In reality, change is a natural part of life. Very little stays the same, so life is a constant adjustment to change. A few "blinders" parents resist change. To avoid change they only see the good in their children, which allows them to avoid making changes in their children's flaws.

Commentary

Imagine the pressure children feel when viewed as perfect by their parents. Consider all the potential difficulties that can arise if children start to believe they have no flaws. Many overindulged children become rigid, forcing their beliefs of perfection onto others.

Many overindulged children do not receive honest advice on how to correct their flaws. When a teacher approaches these children to correct their flaws by mentoring them, these children do not cooperate. They do not know how to have a mutual relationship. Instead, they become indignant or avoid the teacher.

The "Glorifying" Parent

"Glorifying" parents have the wonderful quality of complimenting others. "Glorifying" parents are similar to parents with "blinders," as they ignore their children's flaws; however, "glorifying" parents are different from parents with "blinders" in one major way. "Blinders" parents have an accurate understanding of their children's talents, but ignore their children's flaws. "Glorifying" parents exaggerate their children's talents or see incredible qualities within their children that do not really exist.

Their children mystify "glorifying" parents, who believe that everything their child touches turns to gold. They believe their child has the best personality, the best job, and the best friends. Their child is the best of all.

Julie would constantly boast about her children. They had no equals in her mind. If her teenager got a job, no matter how menial, it was the best job in the world. When her adult children bought a home, there was no equal to their new residence.

To continue glorifying her children, Julie would gloss over real problems. Some of her children became so self-centered they were having difficulties keeping friendships at school. One of her children was convicted as a felon, selling drugs to minors. Julie swept it out of her mind. Julie's adult children were in incredible debt, but she never mentioned it.

When her friends discussed their children, Julie immediately went into competition by bragging about her children. Julie lost friendships because she could not enjoy the successes of her friends' children.

One of Julie's daughters, Cara, was having difficulty at school. Cara could not understand why some of her classmates wanted to fight with her. Like her mother, Cara had a habit of bragging, and would readily point out the flaws of others, embarrassing her classmates.

Unlike her mother, Cara's classmates were not willing to glorify Cara. They did not accept the idea that Cara was incredible. Instead, they believed that she was obnoxious. Being children, they did not handle this problem well, and started to fight with Cara. Cara's glorification by her mother led her to believe she was perfect. But, the real world did not accept Cara's glorified image.

Why would parents inaccurately glorify their children?

The Distorted Beliefs of "Glorifying" Parents:

1. Some "glorifying" parents feel they are living a mundane life. Because they are not happy with their life, their children are handy targets for glorification.

    Julie, Cara's mother, needed a life with real purpose in it. To do a complete job of parenting, she needed to address Cara's real flaws. Instead, Julie helped Cara create a self-centered attitude.

2. In other families, one parent glorifies their children, while the other parent has a more accurate picture. The "glorifying" parent appears to be the better parent, while the more realistic parent seems too critical.

    Jerry and Diane were parents of three children. Jerry would often glorify his children and did not acknowledge their flaws. Diane had a more accurate view. She loved her children enough to look at their flaws and help them make corrections. Jerry could not do this, so he continued to glorify his children, while Diane discussed their real concerns. As Diane would approach the children to address real concerns, Jerry would intervene. He stopped Diane from helping their children correct their flaws, painting a picture of Diane as the nasty parent and promoting himself as the nice parent. Jerry manipulated their relationship into a competition, getting his children to align with him.

Jerry and Diane eventually divorced. Jerry became a holiday parent and Diane continued to help her children with their real concerns. As the children matured into adult life, they developed a more meaningful relationship with Diane, who had always offered the truth. Eventually, most children know what they need and come to appreciate parents who give them quality and realistic lessons in life.

Commentary

Because we love our children, it is easy to glorify them. But when we have an unrealistic view, we create self-inflated, ego-centric children. Let me share an example:

I once counseled a girl named Nicki, who was a bright child, but not gifted. Her parents glorified her and would often call her gifted.

When she entered school, her parents convinced Nicki that she would easily be at the top of her class. When it became obvious that her skills were average, Nicki's parents placed more pressure on her to succeed. When Nicki received grades that were less than "A" quality, she became disruptive in her classroom with tears and tantrums.

Nicki had accepted her parents' unrealistic belief. This inaccurate assessment—that she was gifted—was hurting her honest understanding of herself, and manifested itself in unacceptable behavior. She was not ready for a real world that honestly told her, "Hey Nicki, you are a great person, but you have average intelligence." Nicki needed her parents to mentor her with truth and honesty.

The "Favoritism" Parent

Favoritism parents have the excellent qualities of preference and discrimination, but they distort these qualities by preferring only one of their children. Their preferential overindulgence of one child is so extreme that they neglect their other children, who realize favoritism exists and usually become angry. What's interesting is that, as young children, they rarely become angry with the parent who is offering the preferential favoritism. Instead, they become angry with the favored child.

Jamie was the oldest and preferred child in her family of three children. It was obvious to her sister and brother that their mother preferred Jamie. Her mother always laughed harder when Jamie told a funny story, and cried harder when Jamie was hurt. Jamie's brother and sister recall countless memories of Jamie getting more attention, affection, activities, gifts, and everything.

Not only did Jamie's brother and sister become angry with Jamie; they also started to detach from their mother. As this problem grew into adulthood, every holiday, birthday, and special family event became a time of conflict. As Jamie's brother and sis-

*ter became adults, they found their attempts to build
relationships with Jamie and their mother fruitless.*

*Ruth's children were adults. It was obvious that
she preferred her youngest daughter above the rest of
her children. She showered this daughter with attention, advice, and money. Lots of money! In fact, Ruth's
daughter had a home with all the trimmings she could
never afford, if it were not for Ruth. Ruth also gave
advice to her daughter and son-in-law. Lots of advice!
Marital advice, financial advice, child-rearing
advice, and even advice about sex. Too much advice!
But Ruth's daughter and son-in-law never complained to Ruth, because they were too financially
dependent on her.*

Why would parents play favorites at the expense of
their other children?

The Distorted Beliefs of "Favoritism" Parents:

1. Some "favoritism" parents over-identify with the
child they prefer. For example, a shy parent may over-
identify with the child who is too shy or with the child
who is very social. This over-identification promotes a
quick attachment between parent and child, which does
not occur with the other children.

Sometimes a parent may have a favorite hobby (such
as dance, football, or soccer) and the child who excels
in this preferred hobby becomes the favored one.
Whatever the link, these parents naturally favor one
child above the rest.

Jamie's mother was shy, and Jamie's social gregariousness was attractive to her. As a result, Jamie's mother was living a life she always wanted, but she was living it through Jamie. This vicarious life became so enticing that she ignored her other children.

2. Other parents who play favorites recognize that one of their children is vulnerable. They assume that their other children do not need as much special care and attention as the vulnerable child does—but they do.

Ruth had many children, but she only offered excessive finances and advice to one child, who was the daughter Ruth believed incapable of managing life. Ruth assumed that her other children were more able to handle their problems and frustrations. They were more able, not because they were innately brighter, but because they learned through Ruth's behavior not to depend on others. When Ruth's other children became more independent, she assumed they did not need her. Ruth believed she was only useful to the child who was incapable. Of course, Ruth had much more than money to offer her children, but rarely did.

3. Some "favoritism" parents are needy. The children who respond best to their parents' neediness get the favored attention. Children learn, mostly by trial and error, how to get their parents' attention, and those children who better read and respond to their parents' needs become favored children. The ones who do not respond to those needs receive less attention.

4. A few "favoritism" parents are replaying their own parents' tendency to show favoritism. Parents not favored in childhood create preferences when they become parents. When a "favoritism" parent prefers one child, the favored child usually offers that parent favorism in

return. Although these parents were least favored when they were children, they are now in charge of dispensing and receiving favoritism. They decide who the favored child is and who is not. In at least the eyes of one child, these parents become favored, a status they could not win in childhood.

Commentary

Favoritism is one of the most destructive family dynamics, in part because so many parents do not even realize they are playing favorites. Therefore, favoritism may last for a lifetime, as children become adults and still compete for their parents' attention. Without counseling, favoritism continues to breed serious family problems.

The "Blaming" Parent

"Blaming" parents have the beautiful quality of protecting their children; however, they believe they are protecting their children's self-esteem by always blaming others for their children's misbehavior. For example, if a teacher has a conflict with a child, "blaming" parents will immediately side with their child and blame the teacher. They do not suspend judgment until they talk to the teacher, but immediately believe their children and are ready to blame any opposing party. They rarely consider their children's responsibility for a conflict.

"Blaming" parents often blame one teacher for destroying their children's lives or blame other children for ruining special events. The result is that children who are led to believe they are blameless never learn to manage conflict. Instead, they learn to blame others.

Ally knew she slacked off on her studies in her last semester of her senior year, putting her college scholarship in jeopardy. She knew she was failing calculus. Instead of telling her parents that she was responsible, she started to monster-build her calculus teacher.

She would spend many hours complaining about her calculus teacher's unfairness and favoritism for other students. She even told her parents that her calculus teacher changed grades for certain favored students, which was a lie. When Ally's parents received Ally's grades, they became angry because they knew Ally had lost her scholarship. But they were not angry with Ally. They were angry with Ally's calculus teacher. Believing everything that Ally said about her calculus teacher, they went to the school principal and tried to get the teacher fired. To this day, they blame the teacher for Ally's loss of her scholarship. The teacher had given Ally the grade she had earned. The teacher was doing his job!

At another school, on senior day, high school seniors attacked their school building and destroyed school property. The school administration decided that these seniors exhibited unpredictable behavior, so the students were barred from attending graduation ceremonies. Several parents were upset with the school administration's discipline, but they understood their children deserved this tough consequence. Other parents said, "Not attending graduation ceremonies will scar my child's self-esteem for life." These parents became angry at the school administration, claiming that their discipline was too harsh.

Why would parents want to blame others and never correctly see their children's responsibility for a bad experience or conflict?

The Distorted Beliefs of "Blaming" Parents:

1. If a family of six blames someone outside their family, six people are off the hook. These six people never have to consider their contribution to any problems. It makes them feel more comfortable to blame someone else, instead of taking responsibility in life.

   When parents blame others, they can avoid personal responsibility and the discomfort of change. "Blaming" parents rarely hold their children responsible for their actions. For example, instead of getting upset with their children for attacking the school building, "blaming" parents assume the school administration was too harsh with its discipline. They rarely consider, "If sixteen seniors came to my home and destroyed my property, would I want them to come to a special celebration in my home, one week later?" Instead, they inaccurately conclude, "My child's self-esteem will crumble if he (or she) cannot attend high school graduation." This is not true. If these seniors lose their attendance at high school graduation, and parents reinforce the discipline by saying, "You earned this consequence," then these seniors will learn to behave.

2. Some "blaming" parents have an unusual strain of the "glorifying" parent. They glorify their children, seeing them as too perfect to be responsible for any problem. These parents automatically assume that if their children misbehave, they have valid reasons.

Ally's parents viewed her as too perfect to lie about her calculus teacher, although she did. Her parents' distorted belief of Ally's perfection led them to assume that Ally was telling the truth about her calculus teacher, preventing them from accepting her calculus teacher as a valid source of information. This, of course, stopped her parents from getting at the truth.

Commentary

When parents blame others, they promote the illusion of the 'bad guy,' which is a person who has no good qualities. I equate it to an old Gene Autry western from the 1950s, where the bad guys were completely bad. They had no good features, so it was permissible for the hero to do whatever was necessary to save the day. "Blaming" parents immediately create a completely bad picture of anyone who is in conflict with their children. This allows "blaming" parents to feel justified in taking any action to rescue their children.

"Blaming" parents are not teaching children that conflict is a two-way street, with responsibility for all involved. For example, one mother repeatedly argued with the school principal that her son did not start a fight at school. Since the opposing child started the fight, this "blaming" mother labeled the opposing child as the 'bad guy.' Since he was a 'bad guy,' she believed it was acceptable for her son to fight back. In coaching this mother, I helped her recognize that two decisions had occurred: The opposing child decided to fight—and her child also decided to fight. Both children made a bad decision and both needed discipline.

The "Overly-Responsible" Parent

Like "blaming" parents, "overly-responsible" parents have the valuable quality of protection, but they have a different way of distorting it. "Overly-responsible" parents do not blame others for their children's misbehaviors. Instead, they always blame themselves.

When they blame themselves, they stop their children from taking responsibility for their actions. In fact, if "overly-responsible" parents believe they are the cause of their children's misbehavior, they see no reason to discipline their children. This allows their children to continue to misbehave, without correction.

Glenda would constantly make excuses for her son, Kenny, every time he misbehaved, saying, "It's my fault Kenny is like that." Kenny did anything he pleased. If he wanted something, he would steal it. If another child was in his way, he would push the child. He would spout off to his teacher. No matter what he did, his mother would say, "It's my fault Kenny is like that." All children misbehave, so it is not Glenda's fault every time Kenny acted inappropriately. It is Glenda's fault if Kenny's misbehavior continues undisciplined, as Glenda only keeps explaining, "It's my fault Kenny is like that." At some point, Glenda's unwillingness to discipline will be responsible for Kenny's continued misbehavior.

"If I had not gotten divorced, he would not be in this trouble today," Roberta said, after her son, Mike, was arrested for shoplifting. She never held Mike responsible for his actions, because she always blamed herself. She only held herself responsible

*because she believed that her decision to divorce
had ruined her son's life. Although I would love to see
divorce go away, if it were true divorce created crime,
imagine how many children would be in prison. There
are many children with divorced parents who never
consider committing a crime. Divorce does not help,
but it is not solely responsible for criminal behavior.
Mike is making bad decisions.*

Why would parents blame themselves and not hold
their children responsible for their misbehavior?

The Distorted Beliefs of "Overly-Responsible" Parents:

1. Some "overly-responsible" parents were scapegoats of
   their own childhood families. Their family would
   always blame them for every problem when they were
   children, so they continue to accept this role with their
   own family, always taking responsibility for their children's misbehavior. Glenda was the scapegoat of her
   family when she was a child. As she grew up, taking
   blame was a way of life. She naturally continued her
   self-blaming as she raised her own children.

   Often parents who self-blame place too much
   importance on one reason (such as divorce), never considering the full picture. Every time her son
   misbehaved, Glenda would not consider the full picture
   of all the reasons that contributed to her son's misbehavior. Instead, she only blamed herself, and never
   disciplined her son.

2. Becoming a mentoring parent is a commitment that
   requires making a change in lifestyle. Some parents are
   resistant to making changes. For them, there is safety in

blaming themselves for their children's misbehavior because it is a parenting style that does not require change. They just continue with the unchanging thought, "It is all my fault."

3. Some "overly responsible" parents have the belief, "If I take responsibility, I am helping my child." This offers a false sense of empowerment. When a parent takes the blame for a child's misbehavior, that child will often feel relief. An "overly-responsible" parent will feel empowered when their child feels this relief, but it is false empowerment because the child does not learn to change his or her behavior.

This was the problem with divorced Roberta, whose child shoplifted. She believed that if she took the blame, she gave relief to her child. In reality, she was losing control of her child.

Commentary

When "overly-responsible" parents take the blame for their children's misbehavior, their children do not take responsibility for their actions. This stops children from changing their behavior.

The "Ultimately Responsible" Parent

"Ultimately responsible" parents offer a different twist, which is confusing to children. "Ultimately responsible" parents unpredictably explode with anger. They rage at their children and then take it all back by blaming themselves. This creates confused children who become tense, especially when discussing any family issues that might ignite emotions. They are fearful their parents will rage again, and these children will do anything to avoid their parents' tirade. This stops families from discussing any emotionally-sensitive issues. After the tirade, these parents feel guilty, and overindulge their children, hoping to compensate for the damage created by their tirade.

Tim had a bad temper, made worse by its unpredictability. Usually he was calm, but occasionally he severely blew up without warning. Most of the time, Tim was a good father, but just when his children would start feeling comfortable around him, his anger would unexpectedly explode. Afterwards, guilt-ridden, he would take his children shopping at their favorite toy store, where he overindulged them. But he never fixed his anger, nor did he teach his children that they were not the source of his anger. Instead, he just overindulged them.

Why would parents angrily blame their children, and then try to reverse this by overindulging their children?

The Distorted Beliefs of "Ultimately Responsible" Parents

1. Some "ultimately responsible" parents are so passive that they do not manage their lives. They lack assertiveness, allowing others to mistreat them. This creates a brewing anger within them. By not asserting themselves, "ultimately responsible" parents become frustrated and eventually explode. They unleash their anger on their children, who are the safest targets. Since they often realize (after the blow up) their children are not the real source of their anger, they overcompensate by indulging their children.

2. Some "ultimately responsible" parents are legitimately angry with their children, but choose not to express it. Instead of learning to appropriately communicate their upset feelings, they withhold their hurts and allow them to brew. Of course, these brewing emotions eventually ignite into rage.

Commentary

Without assertiveness, life becomes frustrating. One common feature of people who lack assertiveness is that they harbor considerable anger, which grows as others, including loved ones, continue to take advantage of them.

Parents with frustrated anger, coupled with nonassertiveness, may release their anger toward safe targets—their children. These unpredictable explosions create insecurity for children. Because nonassertive parents have brewing anger, any minor conflict can result in a raging outburst. When these outbursts occur, children learn to restrain their emotions, avoid any potential conflicts, and never discuss emotional issues. The problem escalates when children become teenagers, since most teenagers experience at least one big emotional issue they will need to manage.

Summary

Indulgent parents are basically good-hearted and loving parents who want to be close to their children. But their tendency to overindulge prevents them from achieving a strong emotional bond with their children. I have always found it encouraging that indulgent parents really care about their children, because they are willing to learn and make changes in their parenting in order to build stronger, healthier relationships with their children.

Hope and change lie within the knowledge of identifying the problem. Chapter 2 will help us identify the exact problem. You will also become aware of more major indulgent parenting beliefs that do not work.

~ CHAPTER 2 ~

The Distorted Beliefs of Overindulgent Parents

I am not sure if parenting experts promoted the indulgent parenting beliefs or if parents have misinterpreted what parenting experts have written. It is probably a little of both. However it happened, these are parenting beliefs that overindulgent parents in our culture hold dear.

Many parents assume these distorted beliefs will lead them to a loving relationship with their children. Unfortunately, I do not believe these beliefs are helpful because they usually create more problems than solutions for parents.

Consider each of the indulgent parenting beliefs that follow carefully, because they invariably lead parents to believe they will achieve greater bonding with their children. These distorted parenting beliefs don't work, and I believe parents should be aware of them.

Overindulgent Belief # 1: Constant Happiness

Indulgent parents believe they can heighten their children's self-esteem if their offspring are constantly happy.

Parents push the indulgent belief of constant happiness, for two reasons:

1. They want their children to be constantly happy.

2. They don't want their children to experience any uncomfortable emotions.

Overindulgent parents believe their purpose in life is to give their children a steady stream of fun and happy experiences. Since they believe painful emotions will destroy their children's self-esteem, they will do anything to stop their children from experiencing painful emotions and to stay happy.

While it is admirable for parents to want to increase their children's positive self-esteem and decrease their painful experiences, these efforts to provide what I call a *quick-fix happiness* need to be reconsidered. The marketing definition of q*uick fix happiness* suggests that being a good parent equals the number of happy experiences parents can provide for their children. As a result, parents try to fill every conceivable hour in a child's day with happiness. When you try to push a constant stream of happy experiences onto your children, you will most likely be disillusioned with the outcome.

When parents focus obsessively on their children's happiness, their parenting becomes constricted and ineffective. They believe their sole purpose as a parent is to constantly pursue *quick-fix happiness* for their children.

I counseled two loving parents who were classic over-indulgers. They sent their son to a "fun" day-care. Several times a week, they scheduled "happy" activities. For example, they took him to McDonald's almost every weekend for a Happy Meal. They believed they were strengthening their son's self-esteem by constantly exposing him to happiness.

When their son entered school, he started to have serious behavior problems. It became obvious that they had missed vital ingredients in their parenting! Their son was so egotistical he had not learned to share, cooperate, sacrifice, or take turns with other children. Due to his parents' overindulgence, he had lost many opportunities to learn how to manage life. Instead, he had become an expert on the art of being overindulged.

Why would parents constantly push the quick-fix "marketing" definition of happiness onto their children?

1. Buying happiness has become an art form! In our American culture, providing happy items like toys, fun activities, and Happy Meals is easy, convenient, and quick! Parents do not have to drive far to purchase "happy moments" for their children.

    When you overindulge your children, you do not provide the deeply invested parenting that is necessary to raise them.

2. A common theme in today's culture is the Burger King slogan, "Have it your way." Many adults want happiness in every part of their lives (career, money, advancement, expensive cars, marriages, and children). "I want" is the American dream of our times. When applied to parenting, "I want" does not work as an effective style.

It is a myth to believe children exist to fulfill the needs of parents. Rarely do people with "I want" attitudes think about what is best for the child before having children. Instead, they believe they can work their children into their busy "I want" lifestyles. They convince themselves that if their children are happy, they are good parents. They send their children to a happy daycare and many other happy activities, so they can limit their own involvement with their children.

This allows parents to give up their personal responsibility for raising their children. They can continue with their "I want" lifestyle, falsely believing their children are happy. Unfortunately, by the time their children become teenagers, they are often detached from their parents and ripe for problems that demand considerable parental attention.

Giving the responsibility for raising their children to others gives absentee parents a built-in scapegoat. If "blaming" parents allow substitutes to raise their children, and their children become delinquent, the substitutes are held responsible. The "blaming" parents are off the hook!

Many "I want" parents say they both need to work to provide a good home where they can raise happy children. They use their intentional absenteeism to justify sending their children away from their home to a daycare or babysitter, without realizing the implications or the irony of this action.

Some families have such low incomes that both parents need to work just to survive. Survival is the priority. But there are also two-parent families with good incomes who want the extra spendable income that two careers offer. Whatever the reason, the results are often the same. Without at least one parent actively engaged in parenting, children will not have the benefits of a mentoring parent.

Consider the unique gifts that only you can offer your children. For example, let's pretend that I am your child's daycare worker. One day your child scrapes a knee and cries in agony. As the day care worker, I could hug your upset child ten times and those ten hugs would not be as healing as one hug from you. The caress of your familiar embrace heals your child's pain. That is one little piece of genuine happiness—your children knowing you will be there when they experience pain. Parenting needs to happen when a child needs parenting. No substitute child care advocate can replace this special bond.

How do children react to parents who push them toward constant happiness?

Parents believe their children will react to overindulgence with thoughts like, "Wow, this is great! I love and appreciate my parents!" This rarely occurs. Instead, children more typically respond with feelings of entitlement and resentment.

Instead of learning genuine happiness, overindulged children learn to expect more fun activities, leniencies, and luxuries from their parents. They become indulgent beneficiaries and expect constant attention and entitlement. They eventually have the same expectations of their school and community. Their resentment also ignites, because whenever a child is dependent on a parent, resentment is not far behind. Of course, this is not what overindulgent parents want. These parents are perplexed by their children's strong feelings of entitlement ("I want more") and resentment ("and I'm angry about it"). I can tell you from years of coaching and counseling, overindulgence does not create happy children.

Overindulgent Belief # 2: "Whatever You Want!"

*Overindulgent parents believe that uncondi-
tional love means children should receive
whatever they want and do whatever they want.*

Parents who embrace this indulgent belief have two
major concerns:

1. They have difficulty saying "No" to their children. In
   fact, they measure how good they are as parents by how
   many times they say "Yes" to their children. They
   believe that being a good parent includes buying, giving, leniency, entertaining, and cultivating low
   expectations of their children.

2. Parents who define unconditional love as "giving" luxuries and freedoms have difficulty distinguishing
   between their children's wants (desire for luxuries) and
   their children's needs (love, affection, honesty, etc.).

Indulgent parents give in to all of their children's requests,
which results in overindulged children being out of control in
their families. Parents harboring the distorted definition of
unconditional love as constant "giving" usually overindulge
every whim of their children. Parents who risk 18% interest on
credit card debt to give their children whatever they want are
giving distorted unconditional love. They are actually training
their children to overburden their parents.

Why would parents want to accept this excessive "giving" definition of unconditional love?

1. Some parents overindulge their children to prove to
   themselves and others that they are good parents. They
   have demonstrated their worthiness, because their children have many luxuries and freedoms.

This "Do Whatever You Want" belief is a strong pressure for overindulgent parents who believe that a buddy relationship with their children is a bond. They do not realize that their commitment to be a buddy means losing their parental influence with their children. In their attempts to be buddies with their children, they sacrifice vital tools necessary in raising children. Buddies do not discipline buddies. Buddies are not legally responsible for their buddy's behavior. Buddies do not influence buddies the way parents influence their children. When parents become buddies with their children, they give up their influence!

2. When they say "Yes" to children, indulgent parents feel wonderful. They are convinced they are good parents. Overindulgent parents are happiest when their children are smiling after hearing "Yes" to yet another luxury or fun activity.

On the other hand, some children can make a "want" for a luxury sound like a "need." For example, most children ask for their own television in their bedroom. Indulgent parents have difficulty determining if a television is a "want" or a "need." When parents confuse a "want" and a "need," they are easy marks for manipulative and spoiled children.

A need is anything that sustains life and relationships: such as love, affection, food, shelter, safety, honesty, hugs. Wants are desires for luxuries: televisions, expensive shoes, designer clothes, stereos, a trip to Disneyland, cars, et cetera. Children do not need "luxuries" to have good relationships with their parents. The proof for that last statement is that many families with few luxuries can have very good relationships. Luxuries are not a requirement for good relationships.

How do children react to parents who excessively "give" instead of offering quality parenting?

Children with parents who give them everything they desire push for more! Their parents truly love them, but mistakenly believe that excessive giving will prove their love. They hope their children will reciprocate with love. Instead, these children demand more luxuries and fun activities. Sadly, these overindulged children do not build loving relationships. Instead, they create strong feelings of entitlement ("I want more!"). These children continue to push their parents for more and more expensive items. If parents resist, indulged children become angry.

Children need so much more than luxuries and fun activities from their parents. Children do not always realize that they need love, bonding, discipline, and limits—but they do. When you offer limits to your children, you need to use the word "No" and make it one of the most important words in your vocabulary.

When overindulged children hear the word "No," they refuse to accept it. Instead, they sulk, nag, whine, play guilt trips, and generally make life miserable. Many of these children realize that their overindulgent parents' first "No" is not their final answer. So they whittle their parent's firm "No" into a "Maybe" and eventually into a "Yes." Not only do overindulged children have strong feelings of entitlement, they actively learn how to convince their parents to continue to overindulge them.

Overindulged children never learn to be self-reliant. Instead, they refine their skills of getting what they want from others, without earning it. Instead of self-reliance, they wallow in overdependency. Their only coping skill is the attitude: "You get it for me."

Overindulgent Belief # 3: Shielded From Consequences

Overindulgent parents shield their children from the consequences of their children's actions as well as the complications of life.

Parents who embrace this indulgent belief have two areas of concern:

1. Indulgent parents do not understand the concept of "harm's way." Although parents should stop their children from life-threatening experiences that may result in severe physical or psychological consequences, they overcompensate by protecting their children from the consequences of all their actions, harmful or not.

2. Indulgent parents love to pamper their children. They believe in the "marketing" definition of happiness, suggesting that good self-esteem is the result of keeping their children happy. So, they buffer their children from the consequences of their actions to keep them happy. Since consequences make their children uncomfortable, overindulgent parents harbor the distorted belief that all consequences (even appropriate consequences) create severe psychological harm for their children. This distorted belief drives overindulgent parents to stop their children from receiving consequences for their misbehavior.

If you shield your children from the consequences of their misbehavior, you will create serious problems! If children do not receive consequences for their misbehavior, they will not gain self-guidance. Children create self-guidance when they attach good thinking to their emotions. Consider the example I used in Chapter 1 of good thinking attached to an uncomfortable emotion. If you are at work and you do something that embarrasses you, you can combine this uncomfortable emotion with good thinking, which helps you conclude "I won't do this again at work." This is self-guidance, which is a self-directed willingness to follow rules. For children, self-guidance influences the development of conscience. If their self-guidance is poorly developed, their conscience is also poorly developed.

School administrators enforced the rule that football players arrested for drinking would have to sit out for several games. The students knew the policy and realized it applied to all students in any school activity. It was a logical rule that enforced the idea that students need to use good self-guidance if they want to keep playing football. Their commitment to the team included a commitment to the school's DWI policy.

When parents heard the school administration's decision to follow this policy, they went through the roof! Many parents came to school board meetings with attorneys, to fight the policy. The argument these parents used was, "You are hurting my child's self-esteem with your harsh policy." These parents did not understand the concept of "harm's way."

"Harm's way" is an important parenting principle. Overindulgent parents try to buffer teenagers from the consequences of their actions because they believe it will hurt their children's self-esteem. In reality, these parents are putting their children in "harm's way." If the parents of drinking football players successfully eliminate the school's consequences, they will be teaching teenagers that they can continue to drink alcohol without consequences.

If parents buffer their children from the consequences of their actions, children see no reason to change their misbehavior. They will not create self-guidance that says, "Hey, I better not do that." Instead, overindulged children learn, "I can do what I want and my parents will rescue me from the consequences of my actions." Parents who encourage this attitude are setting their children up for a bigger fall in life, and are putting their children in "harm's way." These children are not developing a conscience!

Why would parents buffer their children from the consequences of their misbehavior?

1. Most parents want to be heroes in their children's lives. Indulgent parents achieve false hero status by rescuing their children from the consequences they deserve.

2. Some parents want to keep their children as children, no matter how old they become. Many parents mourn every passage as their children become adults. For example, when their toddlers are no longer toddlers, most parents mourn that they no longer have toddlers. When teenagers leave home, many parents suffer from the empty nest syndrome. Overindulgent parents suppress their feelings of loss by keeping their children overdependent. As a result, their children never become independent and self-reliant, and cling to their parents even as adults.

What happens when parents buffer the blows of children's misbehavior?

Children who never get guidance or experience consequences for their misbehavior lose the skills of managing life. Everyone's life eventually has complicated issues. That is the way life is. Psychologically healthy adults gradually learn the skills to manage their life and its complications, as they progress from childhood, through adolescence, and into adulthood. Few overindulged children learn the self-management skills they need to manage their life.

To manage problems, parents need to teach children:
* to recognize that a problem exists.
* to consider their contribution to the problem.
* to fix the problem and make amends.

When overindulgent parents buffer their children, their coddled children do not gather the skills to manage life, including solving problems, getting along with others, being responsible and honest, and so much more. These are skills they will need as adults, when parents are no longer able to fix their children's problems.

Children have three distinct reactions when indulgent parents buffer them from the consequences of their behavior: dependency, a lack of age-appropriate skills, and an inflated self-image. This set of reactions perplexes children. On the one hand, overindulgent parents inflate their children's self-image by talking about their positive qualities. On the other hand, these children have no skills, because their parents are doing everything for them.

This creates a Catch-22 dilemma. Overindulged and dependent children become resentful toward their parents, but they have no skills to achieve independence. Dependency and resentment continue to grow until there is an eventual breakdown in parent/child relationships. Often these dependent children stay dependent, but become emotionally distant with their parents. Why?

When a child misbehaves and a responsible parent disciplines that child, the parent teaches the child responsibility. For example:

A ten-year-old boy carved his name on his school desk. The school principal disciplined him. The next day, the child's father accompanied his son to school to repair the desk. This mentoring father taught his son how to sand, stain and varnish the desk. For the next two evenings, this father came back to the school so his son could apply two more coats of varnish. The teacher and school principal praised the boy for the great work he had done.

The father disciplined his son, but he also taught his son how to make a physical, material, and emotional investment in the school. Overindulgent parents do not require their children to make any type of investment, so overindulged children become emotionally distant.

Overindulgent Belief # 4: Sting-Free Discipline

Overindulgent parents either offer no discipline or take the sting out of the discipline they give.

Parents who take the sting out of discipline use a pop psychology idea that I believe can, at times, be a very sabotaging parenting tactic. Parenting experts often suggest that when children misbehave, parents should address their children's misbehavior, but separate the children from their behavior by refraining from criticizing them. So if Johnny lies, he is not a liar. Instead, Johnny is a good child who has a bad lying behavior.

This concept is helpful for parents who verbally abuse their children. It forces parents to stop the abusive labeling by focusing on children's behavior. In other cases, I believe this idea is a saboteur because it takes the sting out of discipline. I am also concerned this parenting technique may create irresponsible children. Often coupled with this idea is another saboteur: Parents who offer sting-free discipline do not apply labels to their children because they believe negative labels hurt their self-esteem. That is true if the negative labels come with no mentoring.

Here is a concern. When does a child who lies become a liar? When does a child who steals become a thief? This is confusing to children. Are they liars when they lie or nice children who lie a lot? Are they thieves when they steal or nice children who exhibit stealing behavior? If a teenager came into your home and stole all of your cherished possessions, what would you call that teen: A nice teen who steals—or would you call that teen a thief? Most of us would call the intruder a thief.

For younger children, heavy labels are obviously harmful. Younger children get into all kinds of mischief as they learn the rules of the world. To label them would be unfair and possibly, self-fulfilling. But as children become older, they need to develop a sense of right and wrong, and recognize the impact of consequences. Labels help do this.

Consider the issue of a person's reputation. Everyone uses labels to describe someone's reputation. For example, if people were to describe you, they would use labels which apprise others of your reputation. Without labels, no one could describe you as having a good or bad reputation.

Reputation is important, and knowing a person's reputation is just as important. If I referred you to a counselor I felt was warm-hearted, generous, disarming, gentle, competent, and dependable, consider your reaction to those labels. What if I described another counselor as threatening, irresponsible, ruthless, and greedy? Consider your ability to trust this counselor with your deepest concerns. Labels give you important information to help you make better decisions. When parents separate children from their behavior and refuse to use labels, they lose the emotional sting of their discipline.

Why does discipline need to have an emotional sting?

Many parenting experts define discipline as a learning experience. Rarely do they discuss children feeling the emotional sting of discipline.

Discipline needs to teach children how to behave, but children should also feel the emotional sting of discipline. For example:

> *Bob's buddy is always disappointing him. His disappointment is an emotional sting—it hurts. His buddy says he is going to come over to play with Bob, but often does not show up. He invites Bob to go to a show, but then goes with someone else, leaving Bob at home.*
>
> *Every time his buddy lets him down, Bob feels the emotional sting of disappointment. This is teaching Bob an important lesson if he applies good thinking to the emotional sting of disappointment: "Never count on this buddy, because he is irresponsible." In fact, if Bob attached further good thinking to his disappointment, he may decide to find a more dependable friend.*

The same lesson is true when children feel the emotional sting of disappointment when they are disciplined. By using good thinking in concert with the emotional sting, the event can motivate them to change.

When overindulgent parents take the emotional sting out of their children's discipline, they stop their children from learning important lessons about themselves. Parents can mentor their children to understand that their painful, but natural emotions have messages. This can lead children to feel empowered to make the necessary changes.

Consider this thought: I am going to give you one of the greatest secrets of influencing children when they are misbehaving. Here it is! *Predict what will happen if they continue to misbehave.* Parental prediction increases your influence with your children, especially as children become teenagers. For example, if your child steals, you can predict that others will label your child as a thief. You can predict for your child that whenever anything is missing, others will accuse him or her of stealing. Then you can predict for your child that getting a reputation (as a thief) will complicate his or her life.

Of course, when your children refuse to listen, allow them to receive the full consequences of their misbehavior. Then, when your prediction comes true, whether children admit it or not, they will realize that you are right. With greater influence, you can guide your children to take better actions.

Why do parents take the sting out of their discipline?

1. Some parents want their children to consider them as "nice." Wanting a reputation of being a nice person, especially with children, is not a bad quality, but parenting is not a popularity contest. Sometimes it demands taking unpopular stances.

   There are times when parents need to be "not nice." Consider this example:

   Teddy was failing at school. He wanted his parents to lie to his grandparents about his failing grades. When his parents refused to lie, he thought they had betrayed him. Their truthfulness seemed like a "not nice" quality, but it was actually a necessary quality, because hiding his grades would misrepresent his poor scholastic achievements and shield him from the feelings of embarrassment. When accompanied by good thinking, embarrassment is an emotional sting that can teach Teddy that he needs to be responsible and study more.

Studying naturally seems painful to many children. If parents want to be considered "nice," they are more likely to let children off the hook when they do not want to study. There are times to be nice and there are times to be firm. Overindulgent parents believe that parenting is a popularity contest. Parenting is not a popularity contest!

2. Some parents ignore their children's imperfections, refusing to face reality. For example, parents see their newborn babies as bundles of beautiful perfection. But I believe God turns babies into teenagers to keep parents humble. As their babies become teenagers, realistic parents change their view of their children to keep a realistic balance. This change of view is a natural part of parenting, because children need to express their God-given talents, which may not include parents' hopes and fantasies. Some parents, stuck in denial, strive to keep their original fantasies alive.

Other parents believe that if they give their children little or no discipline, their children will magically become the fantasy children they hoped for. These parents offer a passive parenting attitude, despite evidence that their children's misbehavior is getting progressively worse.

The major characteristic of parents who are fixated on rearing fantasy children is glorification of their children. As previously mentioned, their children may have the worst job in the world, but "glorified" parents believe their ideal child has the best job in the world.

Their children could be driving a junk heap, but idol-making parents glorify it into the best car in the world.

Although their children are not achieving the fantasy their parents hoped for, these parents ignore reality and preserve a fantasy that their hopes are coming true. As they continue to see their children as perfect, they see nothing to discipline. No discipline means children receive no emotional sting and no mentoring. Without the emotional sting of discipline, they will not develop self-guidance. Without quality self-guidance, children are headed for behavior problems—and struggles throughout life.

Overindulgent Belief # 5: "Highest Priority"

Overindulgent parents believe their children are the highest priority in their family.

Indulgent parents lift their children to the highest priority in their families. This is a major problem! Children should be a high priority in all families, but not the highest priority. The highest priority should be the marital relationship, which is the epi-center of a family.

When one spouse views the other as the highest priority and the other spouse does the same, these couples rarely need marriage counseling! This healthy priority says to a spouse "I will always consider my spouse first in all my thoughts, decisions, and actions." With this shared priority, married couples take care of each other with mutual respect. However, if one or both of them does not make their spouse the highest priority, marital problems may ignite. When this happens, the neglected spouse yearns "My needs, my needs, my needs," because critical needs are not being met in the relationship.

When emotional needs are not met in their marriage, parents often turn to their children. This shift from spouse to child allows children to become the highest priority within their family. This creates critical issues for children, because they are incapable of buffering their parents' marital problems.

Marital problems are not the only issues that allow children to become the highest priority in their families. Unfortunately, overindulgent parents misinterpret the concept of "child-centered" parenting, and use it as an excuse to make children the highest priority of their families. In reality, children do not have the intelligence to be the highest priority of their family. Parents are the only people in families who are capable enough to manage a household and apply their life experiences to the situations which arise. So, when children become the most influential members of their families, under the guise of being the highest priority, their growth and maturation is stunted.

What happens when indulgent parents make their children the highest priority of their families?

When children are the highest priority in their families, indulgent parents shift decision-making responsibilities to their children, which allows children to take charge of their family. The chick is in charge of the henhouse! The tail is wagging the dog!

An example of children's power in "child-centered" families is when parents are willing to sacrifice finances and accumulate extreme credit card debt to give their children luxuries and fun activities. Someone may ask, "Isn't it noble for parents to sacrifice for their children?" It is, when children are in "harm's way" with a life threatening illness or dangerous life experience. In those situations, most parents appropriately make their children the highest priority and would sacrifice everything to save their children. But when parents put their credit rating and retirement in "harm's way" by buying another expensive toy or another fun activity—that is another matter.

A further complication is that siblings are "fairness detectors" with a warped sense of fairness. Children constantly oversee their parents' fairness. With siblings, children monitor and enforce getting their fair share of stuff. Also, children tend to forget everything they get from their parents because they are focused on the "here and now."

When seven-year-old Michelle saw her parents buy her sister a new toy, Michelle did not think, "Yesterday my parents bought me a new toy, so now my sister and I are even. My parents sure are treating us fairly." Instead, Michelle focused on the "here and now" and complained, "Hey, that's not fair. If she is getting a new toy, I should get one too!" Parents who make their children the highest priority will accept Michelle's complaint as legitimate. Michelle convinces her parents, with her narrow definition of fairness, to buy her another toy. Michelle is now in charge! With a child's mind, she becomes the power-center of her family. She decides how fairness works in her family and when her parents should buy her toys.

When parents embrace a child's immature thinking, the goals of the family shift. Michelle does not want to hear her parents explain that she got a gift yesterday, so she should not get a gift today. Her sister received a gift today, so Michelle wants a gift today.

Never be bound by a definition of fairness based on gifts and privileges. Always remember that true fairness offers equal love, not equal gifts. You can love your children equally, but you should raise them differently. Children have different personalities, different temperaments, different reactions to discipline, and countless other differences. Some children are easy to raise and some are not. So, when a parent accepts a child's immature definition of fairness, suggesting that parents should act the same for each child, parents lose empowerment to raise their children as individuals.

When accepting their children's immature definition of fairness, parents dispense expensive rituals of "false-respect" onto their children. For example:

I asked a recent high school graduate where she was going to college and she gleefully replied, "Denver, Colorado." Since this college was out-of-state with expensive tuition, I assumed that she was pursuing a specialized field of study. When I asked her what she was majoring in, she said, "I haven't decided yet." When I asked her why she was going to Colorado she replied, "It's pretty!" Why would her parents pay all that extra money for college, without a special purpose? The answer is—a false, but expensive, ritual of respect. She wants it, she gets it!

What happens to children when they become the highest priority of their families?

The answer is that children attain power, too much power! Power they are incapable of handling. Children need their parents' guidance. When parents do not provide the proper guidance, children feel pressure (or permission) to take charge of their families, striving to prove they are the most powerful person in their families.

Children need to know their limits. Without limits, they pressure parents to yield to childish whims and fancies. When parents offer no or few limits, children realize they are in charge. When they become teenagers without limits, they believe they can do anything. When other authority figures such as teachers, principals, and police officers build in limits with discipline, these teenagers feel no motivation for change. Instead, they become oppositional. Teenagers without limits are like automobiles without steering wheels. They could do anything. Anything!

Bret's mother grew weary of Bret's abusive father. When he drank, he was even more abusive. She talked openly about leaving him, but whenever she mentioned divorce, seven-year-old Bret would become upset and cry. Finally, Bret's mother looked at Bret and said, "I'll leave it up to you. Should I divorce Daddy or not?" Imagine the youngster's reaction to such a complicated grown-up question. Bret answered the way a typical seven-year-old would. He said that he did not want his parents to divorce.

After that conversation, whenever Bret's father became abusive his mother would remind Bret that it was his decision that they did not divorce. Later, when she felt guilty for putting him in such a no-win position, she would use credit cards to indulge Bret. Of course, dad—the angry alcoholic—was always looking for a reason to be angry. So, when he saw the credit card bill, he would beat Bret's mother. Then the indulgent cycle would begin again. Many overindulgent parents want their children to be happy, but use overindulgence as a mask for allowing abuse.

Children who are the highest priority in their family do not have the ability to uphold this lofty status. They lose their childhood and they lose the safety of knowing their parents are creating a healthy family with well-defined limits, a family that children can rely on.

Overindulgent Belief # 6: "Wishy-Washy Decisions"

Overindulgent parents have difficulty with making firm decisions.

Parenting experts suggest that parents negotiate with their children gradually, as they become older. This is a great idea. Parents need to replace control with influence as children become teenagers. Unfortunately, overindulgent parents negotiate every issue with their children, at all ages. Every topic is open for negotiation, even with young children. This creates children who act like attorneys, offering one-sided debates to get the best deal. This is a problem that will only intensify as children become teenagers!

When overindulgent parents waver in their decisions by negotiating with young children, the children realize that no parental decision is ever final. All decisions are negotiable. This becomes a problem because parents and young children have two different goals. When most parents negotiate, they are willing to compromise. When young children negotiate, they want to win. Under these circumstances, parents can easily lose their influence.

Unhealthy negotiation is an example of a parenting skill used at the wrong time. Parents, with good intentions, are negotiating with young children. This results in parents who appear wishy-washy in their decision-making. Unlike younger children, many older children understand that negotiation can result in mutual compromise. So, negotiation often works well when parents negotiate with more mature children.

Why do parents have difficulty making firm decisions?

1. Some parents dislike decision-making and shift it onto others so they can avoid the responsibility that comes with it. At work, they shift decision-making onto fellow employees. In their personal life, they shift decision-making onto their friends. In marriage, they shift their decision-making onto their spouses. In parenting, they shift their decision-making onto their children.

2. Some parents shift decision-making onto children, believing children should have equal status with adults in their family. Children do have equal status, but they do not have equal brainpower. Overindulgent parents give children too much decision-making power, believing they are building children's self-esteem. In reality, when children make decisions before they are capable, they are set up to fail, which damages their self-esteem.

What happens to children with parents who do not make firm decisions?

Parents who make wishy-washy decisions have cildren who are always trying to discover their limits. When everything is negotiable, there are no limits. Children constantly question or push on how far they can go with their behavior.

When children are asked to make decisions they are too young to make, their decisions are usually bad. Many children, forced into adult decisions, either become self-inflated or insecure. As adults, they often view decision-making as a pressure-filled responsibility they would rather avoid. This promotes dependence on others to make decisions for them. They lose the essential life-management skill of making good decisions.

Overindulgent Belief # 7: "Too Trusting"

Overindulgent parents are too trusting.

When parents feel inadequate about their parenting skills, guilt is often the result. The combination of inadequacy and guilt creates parents who are susceptible to their children's guilt trips. To erase their guilt, parents become too trusting of their children. They believe that if they trust their children more, they will feel less guilt and their children will be happy.

Most parents want to believe their children, but children are children and they occasionally misbehave. For example, when children occasionally lie they may use manipulative guilt, suggesting to their parents, "If you were a good parent, you would believe me."

When overly-trusting parents feel guilt, they edit out facts so they can continue to believe their children. If other authorities, such as teachers, principals, or counselors, tell parents the truth about their children, overly-trusting parents discount the advice and support of those authorities.

When children complain about teachers, reserve your judgment until you have all the facts and talk to all parties. While it is important to listen to children's complaints, do not take action too quickly. Instead, do a "round-up" of the essential facts and details in order to make a wise, educated decision.

When your child complains about a teacher, contact the teacher for information about your child's grades and behavior. Next, seek a meeting (round-up) to bring all parties together to explore legitimate concerns. Revealing the truth is easier when a more complete picture emerges. If you discover there is a concern with a teacher, take appropriate action. If the teacher is not the issue and your child is manipulating, discipline the child.

Why are indulgent parents too trusting? Why do they edit out reality, when they hear facts about their children from other authority figures?

1. Some parents are too trusting because they want to equate trust with being good parents. To confirm this belief they decide, "My children are right and everyone else is wrong." This belief leads to complications because it affects others. For example:

    A couple arranged counseling for their teenage daughter with me, because she had vandalized their neighbor's house. When I was taking a history of the girl's background, I asked the standard questions about drug use. I had her tested and found that she had cocaine and heroin in her during the time of the vandalism. When I asked her parents about their concerns with her drug use, they immediately defended their daughter and assured me she was only experimenting with drugs. I told them that I defined drug experimentation as the occasional use of marijuana, and that using cocaine and heroin was far from experimentation. Her parents started to monster-build with me, getting very angry because I would not edit reality. I became the "bad" psychologist because I would not leave reality behind.

    When parents inappropriately attack others to minimize their children's serious misbehavior, they stop themselves from dealing with the reality of their children's misbehavior.

2. Parents who trust too much want to be rescuers for their children. By being rescuers, parents see themselves as good parents in an evil world. They see their children as victims and they readily believe any stories about their children's victim status. This is especially true of parents who harbor anger. Angry parents will easily ally with their children when they are upset. This allows angry parents to unleash their own long-standing anger at targets. Instead of properly managing their anger, they unleash anger at anyone who criticizes their children—even those who have legitimate concerns and proof.

When angry parents unleash their anger at others, they believe they are bonding with their children. What they are actually creating is a dysfunctional alliance. Alliances are not bonds. They are temporary agreements to fend off attack or blame others. Unlike alliances, bonds are deep and permanent commitments based on truth. Alliances can easily shift and break. Bonds are much stronger.

In the earlier example with the drug abuse issue, if one of the parents changes his or her thinking and accepts that there may be a drug problem with their daughter, the other parent is in a bind. If the parents have a true bond, they would consider the possibility of drug abuse for their daughter and support each other. If they have an alliance, it would not be safe for either of them to consider the possibility of drug abuse with their daughter, because the "aware" parent becomes the bad-guy in the eyes of the other parent. When this occurs, conflict often arises with the goal of getting the parent (who is considering the reality of the drug abuse) to get back into an alliance (by avoiding the reality of the drug abuse). Unlike alliances, bonds are based on dealing with truth and reality.

Overindulgent Belief # 8: "I Will Correct My Parents' Mistakes"

Overindulgent parents believe their parents raised them improperly. It is the longing of indulgent parents to correct their own parents' mistakes, by becoming perfect parents.

Parents using this indulgent belief often share this parenting creed: "I shall repair my childhood by replaying my childhood through my children. I shall be a 'child-centered' parent and give my children everything they want to ensure their happiness. I shall be the perfect parent my parents never were. If I do this, I shall be a good parent. We will bond and my children will be happy."

When parents practice this parenting creed, their sole purpose is to erase their own parents' mistakes by preserving the illusion that they will make their children happy by being better parents than the parents who raised them. Instead, these parents often create a new set of mistakes. They raise their children based on parenting they wanted from their own parents, which stops them from realizing the "actual" parenting needs of their own children.

Why is each generation of parents convinced the previous generation did such a bad job of parenting? If the previous generation of parents did such a bad job of parenting, how did this current generation of adults become one of the most advanced in technology, information, education, and enlightenment?

Is the past important? Yes, but the past is no more important than the present and the future. The past cannot change, so true empowerment (which should be the bedrock of counseling) is in the present and its effect is on the future.

Why is it important to review the past?

The past is only part of a large puzzle. It is important to know the impact of the past, but realizing the impact must serve a useful, not destructive, purpose. Adults can stop obsessing about the past by considering all three parts of life (past, present, and future). Consider this empowerment question: *If this happened in the past, what are you going to do about it now?*

Why do parents hurt by their past blame their parents for their own lack of parenting skills? I am going to give you my favorite answer: "I don't know." A more productive path, when adults review their past, is to create a change that improves their present and their future.

Most adults have had a combination of good and bad experiences when growing up, with parents giving loving support, as well as emotional pain. Adults need to know the impact others had on them when they were children. A healthy goal for parents is to understand the strengths and flaws of their own parents. Parents need to embrace the positive qualities of their own parents and actively improve any negative influences. For example, a woman verbally abused by her mother needs to understand the impact of the abuse, which would help her be sensitive to other survivors of abuse. An understanding of the impact of the abuse can encourage her to not repeat the abuse with her children.

When parents feel true emotional pain about their childhood, they need to stop searching for a scapegoat. They can consider a better alternative. Parents can view their own parents as real people with strengths and flaws. This gives parents empowerment, not by angrily obsessing about the past, but by focusing on the present and the future, where empowerment and change reside.

I suggest to parents that if they want to review their own parents' influence, they can do it with a healthy attitude. For example, my father was like any other person with strengths and flaws. When I reviewed my childhood, instead of criticizing my father for his flaws, I searched for what he directly and indirectly taught me. I also considered how to use his lessons today.

What my father taught me, and how I use it today:

1. My father taught me that time spent with children is important. He taught me this, not because he was there much, as he was a typical 1950s–1960s father who worked hard. I now understand his work ethic. I also understand the impact of his limited time at home. This motivates me to spend much time with my children.

2. He could tell colorful stories about the personalities of family members of previous generations, which made me feel connected to them. He was good at this! I am too!

3. He taught me that education is important. He had none and he shared how it affected him through his frustrations and wishes for careers that he never attained. This is one of the greatest lessons he taught me.

4. He taught me not to give up on my dreams, because he often did. You are reading my second book: another dream come true!

5. He taught me to hate 9-to-5 jobs, because he hated his for thirty years.

6. He taught me how important religion was to him by his reluctance to express his religious beliefs for fear of embarrassment. His embarrassment to speak about religion was as strong as his beliefs. I am not afraid to express my religious beliefs.

7. He was an honest person. He taught me to tell the truth and he physically disciplined me when I did not. He was not abusive when he offered a spanking. I earned it and I knew it. I also value telling the truth.

8. He used body language to show love, because he had difficulty saying, "I love you." He taught me to say, "I love you" because he had difficulty saying, "I love you."

9. He taught me to buy a car by not giving me one. Self-reliance is a blessing in any era.

10. When he died, he taught me there is a limit to a life span. I try to use it well.

I could view my father as a neglectful workaholic. I have chosen the mind-set that I want to learn from his strengths and flaws. If I believed my father should have been perfect, then he came up short. The mind-set I choose is to see him as a human father of the 1950s-1960s who did what his times expected, and a man I can learn from to change my present and future life for the better. From his strengths and flaws, I learned lessons that helped me set my priorities. Therefore, the mind-set I have chosen allows me to feel great love for him. Even though he has been dead for years, he is still doing good work today. Thanks Dad!

I regularly advise parents not to worry about passing the bad affects of their own parents on to their children. All parents will have their own unique affects on their children, good and bad. It is helpful if parents have this "learning mindset" when they review their childhood.

Many overindulgent parents believe they have to be perfect in their parenting. They assume this will get them perfect children. Here is one of my own favorite quotes that I offer to all parents:

> **Being a good parent does not mean that you raise perfect children.
> Being a good parent means that you know what to do when your children are not so perfect.**

Overindulgent Belief # 9: "Who Am I And Why Am I Here?"

Overindulgent parents need more identity development, which means they do not know who they are or why they are here.

Indulgent parents need to create their own identities because:

1. Some parents limit their identities to their careers, which are demanding and lessen the time they need to be active in other parts of their lives, such as parenting.

2. Other parents define their identities only by their children's current level of happiness.

People need to understand themselves well before they become parents. Their decision to become parents should come from a deep understanding of themselves.

Identity is a truthful understanding of oneself. To understand this, identity requires:

- realizing your personal strengths and weaknesses;
- having values reflecting decency that are consistent;
- living life to its fullest, with a purpose.

These are requirements that many adults choose to avoid by ignoring personal strengths and weaknesses, having inconsistent values, and not having a purpose in life.

A requirement for identity is a foundation of core beliefs. The best way to discover if you have core beliefs is to consider your opinions about hot controversial topics such as abortion, right to die, or belief in God. If you do not have strong opinions about hot controversial topics, then your identity needs enhancing. When asked about hot controversial topics, adults without firm identities agree with whoever is dominating the conversation.

Parents without identities have struggles helping children create identities for several reasons:

- Children model their parents and if parents have little identity to model, children lose an important resource for the creation of their own identity.
- Some parents do not realize that they exist for a purpose. Having a purpose creates a life with direction.
- Other parents have a dream about what they want to be, but they have not been able to reach it. They never modify their dreams to make them more attainable, so they give up.

Pete was a father who always wanted to be a football player in high school and college. He was big enough and he had a thorough understanding of football strategies. But he was clumsy. He never reached his desire to be a football player, but he loved the game. As an adult, he found himself stuck in a job that did not resemble his interest in football or any other interest.

His son was big and ready for football. Pete was happy to be involved in football again, and his son delighted in receiving all of Pete's attention. Together they practiced football and prepared for tryouts. As they worked together, Pete saw the same irritating clumsiness within his son that he had. He tried to help his son correct these problems, but became more irritated with each failure.

Once when Pete was helping his son practice, his son's clumsiness was unbearable. Pete suddenly became frustrated and violent, pushing his son against their house. He was about to punch his son when his wife intervened. This violent reaction baffled everyone, including Pete, because Pete was not a violent man.

Pete's identity remained with football, although his career went elsewhere. When he saw an opportunity to have his identity back (vicariously through his son), Pete was happy. But when he saw the same frustrating clumsiness emerge from his son, Pete popped a cork. He released his frustrations at his son, because he was reminded of his own flaws.

When Pete entered counseling, I helped him realize that he had decisions to make. He was in a career that did not reflect his true identity, which made him feel empty. Through counseling, he learned that football was a major part of his identity. He knew he had a brain for football. He knew football strategies better than most football coaches.

In a counseling session, he complained that it would take him four years to finish a degree to become a football coach. He sadly said he would be 48 years old, suggesting that it was too late. I advised Pete that he could become 48 years old and happy, or he could become 48 years old and more miserable. Either way, Pete was going to be 48 years old.

Pete went back to school. He is now a high school coach living a dream, instead of bitterly dreaming about life. He loves molding teenagers into adults with his love of football. He is teaching his students about life through football. He has a purpose in life!

Why would people not want to create their own identity?

1. Creating an identity is pleasurable, painful, and requires taking risks in life. Many people appreciate the pleasurable part, but do not care for pain and risk-taking. Risk-taking increases a person's opportunity for success and failure. Many people want to avoid the painful failure of risk-taking, but it is from failures that people learn how to succeed.

   Successful parents have a particular skill that I consider to be one of their greatest assets. When these parents fail, the first thought they have after experiencing failure is "Okay, it does not work this way. How am I going to make it work? What are my choices?"

   I counseled Pete to incorporate this survival skill into his thinking. He wanted to be in football, but he believed he should have been a football player and missed his chance. When he assessed his skills by considering his past, present, and future, he learned to adapt his dreams. He realized that he had all the necessary skills to be a football coach. He learned that if he wanted to enjoy life, he needed to take a bold risk (go back to school to change his career).

He found that change is a bit scary and requires a sacrifice of time, money, and effort. It is a rare person who has an incredibly happy and successful life by chance. Many people sit back and wait to be happy. Pete learned to invest in his life, and is now looking forward to his future.

I often ask parents, "If you were Pete's son, which parent would you rather have as a model to guide your life? Would you prefer a parent who unleashes frustrated anger at you, or would you prefer a parent who knows what he wants and goes after it? Which parent would be a more attractive leader? Which parent would be easier for children to bond with?"

2. When people have identities, they know their values. Values encourage parents to manage all aspects of life. Values require that parents address uncomfortable issues that indulgent parents like to avoid.

When parents have inadequate identities, they also have inconsistent values. Parents with inconsistent values create confusion within their children. What messages do parents send when they reprimand a child for stealing, but then cheat on their taxes? What if grandfather is dead, but a child hears that grandfather is sleeping? In both cases, parents have damaged the value of honesty. Values such as honesty offer a foundation that helps parents create consistency, stability, and predictability in their emotions, thoughts, actions, and relationships.

There are two types of values: **basic values** and **selected values. Basic values** feed children's conscience development. If people do not have basic values, they can become bad people. People select all of their values, but basic values are necessary for everyone. For example, safety is a basic value, one that is vital for quality relationships. When people are together, they assume they will be safe with one another. But what if the basic value of safety does not exist within a family? Without it, close personal relationships fray and deteriorate.

What if the basic value of honesty does not exist within a family? Its absence can destroy relationships. In an era of "Don't tell me what my values are," basic values are becoming more essential than ever before. When people do not have basic values, they do bad things and become bad people.

Selected values are values which people choose with their own priorities. For example, when considering a hot controversial topic such as abortion, one person may prefer the value of personal freedom and be pro-choice. Another person may prefer the value of life and be pro-life. Both are people with selected values, but they have different selected values.

If these two people have the same basic values (safety, honesty, integrity), but different selected values (Pro Choice vs. Pro Life), they can respect each other's views without hostility. If they do not have basic values, they become hostile and may harm each other.

Family members can have different "selected" values and continue to be respectful if they have basic values. If family members do not share "basic" values, the family is in serious jeopardy. When parents do not have "basic" values, serious harm can come to children.

Tommy's father always told ten-year-old Tommy to be honest. Tommy often lied by omitting important information, which upset his father. Tommy's father told Tommy how painful it was when he learned something bad about Tommy, which his own son had neglected to tell him. Tommy's father was teaching him the importance of honesty (a basic value), and that omitting important information was a form of lying.

Unfortunately. Tommy's father deceived his family by having an affair. To conceal his affair, he lied by omission. Tommy's father upheld an image of something he was not, a faithful and honest husband and father. Later, Tommy learned about the affair and realized his father had cheated on both him and his mother.

His father's deception hurt Tommy's ability to trust. Tommy refused to accept all his father's lessons about honesty, loyalty, and basic values. His mother brought him into counseling, because Tommy started to lie, deceive, and manipulate others.

Every time 15-year-old Janelle advocated the right-to-die, her mother became angry. The thought that Janelle would ever consider that taking one's life was acceptable appalled her mother. Janelle's mother believed that if she screamed loud enough, she could force Janelle to change her mind. Janelle did not change her mind. Instead, she decided that her mother was not open-minded enough to talk about hot controversial topics.

When Janelle was 17 years old, she became pregnant. Instead of sharing this emotional situation with her mother, she had a friend take her for an abortion. Her mother never knew about the baby or the abortion.

Tommy's father needed to be consistent with his basic values and realize that an affair is not worth the price of destroying his family. Janelle's mother did not have to agree with Janelle, but rather, realize that Janelle was contemplating "selected" values. Janelle's opinions will change many times before she finally decides about controversial issues. Janelle's mother would have more influence if she created a safe atmosphere for discussing hot controversial issues.

When children learn their parents are safe with hot controversial topics, they are more willing to discuss controversial issues. When parents model basic values (honesty, safety, loyalty), they will remain a positive, powerful influence in their children's lives.

SUMMARY

You now have the major overindulgent beliefs. This is helpful information to use as you consider which parenting skills need to be addressed. Children will misbehave, and it is frightening what little control parents actually have over them. But parents can always have control over their own actions, which can create incredible influence with their children. The guideposts you can effectively use in your parenting are the qualities of the mentoring parents offered in the next chapter.

~ CHAPTER 3: ~

The Qualities of the Mentoring Parent

The qualities of the mentoring parent can solidify families. If you use the qualities of the mentoring parent to replace overindulgence, you will increase your bond with your children.

Becoming a mentoring parent requires changing your understanding of your job as a parent and your purpose in raising children. Your purpose as a parent is to mentor your children. Warning! Your children will initially resist these changes. Children will want overly permissive parents to go back to their old indulgent ways. But if you persist, you will have a wonderful result—a real bond with your children!

The principles of the mentoring parent are not a treatise on parenting theory. Instead, they represent a usable and dynamic style of parenting which is easy to use. While this parenting style is not a political statement, some of its ideas may be challenging for "child-centered" parents.

In my practice, I have seen a shift of family power transfer from parents to children—manipulative and immature children who are devastating their families. The principles offered in this book are not hard to implement. You can become a quality mentor to your children.

Quality #1: "I Will Raise My Children"

Mentoring parents raise their children and do not abdicate their childrearing responsibilities to others.

I want to emphasize emphatically that this is not a political statement to keep mothers at home. It does not matter which parent stays home; the priority is that at least one parent spends considerable time at home, mentoring children. Mentoring parents cannot mentor their children if they are not with them.

Georgia and Bart were unhappy with the results of their parenting. Their daughter was in a quality daycare center. Both Georgia and Bart worked 40-plus hours a week outside their home, and in spite of the quality daycare center, they noticed their daughter was not bonding with them as much as they thought she should.

I asked them to do an experiment, (which is one you can use). I asked them to sit on their front porch and watch neighborhood children coming home from school, then decide which neighborhood children were heading home to a parent and which were going to an empty house. Georgia and Bart easily recognized the difference. The children, going home to an empty house seemed unhappy, out-of-control, or both.

This experiment became a life-changing event for them. They had mentored their daughter when it was

- Can one or both parents earn an income at home?
- Does one parent have the skills to work where their children attend school (for example: secretary, teacher's aid, coach, attendance office, cafeteria, teacher)?
- Can one parent work only when children are attending school?
- Can either parent do e-commerce in their chosen field of work?
- Does one parent earn enough money so the other parent can stay home?
- Did the parents create huge and wasteful debt with a large house payment? Can they reduce their debt?

Consider how to increase the time you spend with your children and reduce your debt, if debt is an issue for you. Many times I counsel families that have serious debt issues which consume their money and force them to spend more time away from home.

Alicia and Philip had a large expensive home with all the amenities. They also had every toy, including a boat, camper, recreational vehicles, and more. But what they had the most of was crippling credit card debt.

They had their two younger children farmed out to an expensive daycare, and their teenagers came home to an empty house. They believed they needed to have this large home to make their children happy. They loved their home, so my suggestion was difficult for them. I suggested they downsize! It was a difficult decision, but they decided to get a smaller home, sell some of their expensive toys, and have a huge garage sale.

One evening when Philip came home from work, Alicia was sitting in the middle of the living room with all their children, plus six of their children's friends. They were eating popcorn and watching a movie. Both realized they had not had the time to do this in their large home because they were too busy paying for it. In the old house, they had multiple televisions, so they did not gather in the same room together. One TV meant togetherness.

There is no substitute for involved parents. Only parents can offer a healing hug to their children and mentor in their own special way. Quality time spent with children is your best investment.

Quality #2: The Whole Truth And Nothing But the Truth!

Mentoring parents have a deep commitment to truth and reality and help their children accept what is joyful as well as what is painful.

Truth is one of the key foundations of a family. Without truth, families crumble. Mentoring parents have a deep commitment to truth. Children need to be able to rely on their parents to always tell them the truth.

Mariam and Jack did not have the heart to tell their seven-year-old son the family dog was hit by a car and killed. So, they let their son believe the dog was missing, but still alive. They hoped to protect their son from the pain of grief, but every night their son would ask them to help him look for the dog.

These protective parents kept their secret and pretended to search for their dead dog. Eventually, in tears, he announced that the dog left because the dog did not like him. His parents' dishonesty led to their son's distorted interpretation of the event. They became co-conspirators in the boy's low opinion of himself.

Mentoring parents work hard to correct children's distorted thoughts and to manage emotions by telling the truth. When parents are not truthful, one lie creates a need for another lie and another. Children need to know that they can trust their parents to tell the truth.

When parents talk to their children, there are two types of messages that happen: a content message and a hidden message. When parents are truthful about an important issue, the content message honestly tells children what occurred. The hidden message of offering the truth to children is the belief that parents and children can work together to manage difficult issues.

Truth is a great foundation for daily communication in families even when painful events occur, if parents are open and honest. If parents are dishonest about painful events, children receive a hidden message that the family cannot manage problems together.

Mentoring parents realize that children need to hear the truth about their good behavior, as well as their misbehavior and limitations. They offer this feedback in a caring and genuine manner. If parents give children inaccurate and dishonest feedback, they set up their child for problems.

Tony's parents often told Tony, "You are gifted." Since Tony was young, his dad spent enormous time with Tony, which sounds like a great investment. But Tony's dad was trying to mold Tony into something he

*was not. He wanted a gifted child and had worked
toward that goal since Tony was an infant. Tony
started to believe in his giftedness. In reality, he had
average intelligence and attended a school which
would recognize his average intelligence.*

*Tony had a difficult time adjusting to the idea that
he had average intelligence. Since his father did not
give him an accurate reflection of his skills and abilities, Tony had to deal with a distorted image, which
complicated his life.*

Mentoring parents never exaggerate their children's
strengths or ignore their limits. Children need to know that
they can always count on their parents to give them truthful
information, in a direct but caring manner. Anything less is
a recipe for failure! Tony needed a mentoring parent who
would accept him as he was and help him progress as far as
he could go. Many average children become exceptional
adults if they are taught to honestly understand themselves.

Mentoring parents never keep secrets, because secrets
destroy family relationships. It is amazing how children
learn about family secrets. They are "truth detectors"—
sponges that absorb every conversation not meant for them.
They overhear telephone conversations or have siblings and
cousins tell them the rest of the story. They notice subtle
changes in their parents when certain topics arise.

When children realize their parents have a secret, their
distrust brews. They wonder what other secrets exist. When
secretive parents discuss important family issues, children
wonder if they are hearing a full story. When parents keep
secrets, it forces them to deceive their children, which stops
honest and wholesome family bonding. Mentoring parents
do not keep secrets, and are prepared to discuss sensitive
issues.

The problem with dishonesty and secrets is that they require continued lying. Liars forget and become inconsistent. So, it is important that parents tell their children the truth. Mentoring parents know that truthfulness creates consistency, because truth reflects reality. Lies become obvious over time and children need dependable, consistent and honest parents. Mentoring parents strive to be consistent and truthful.

Rationalizations For Not Being Truthful with Children:

One rationalization overindulgent parents believe is that a lie will protect the children from emotional pain. In the previous example with the missing dead dog, the boy eventually heard from a friend that his dog was dead and that his parents knew the dog was dead. His parents were unaware he had learned the truth about his dog, and a deceptive wedge of dishonesty came between these parents and their child. The parents continued their deception, but their son recognized their deceptiveness. To retaliate, every night this boy would ask his parents to help him look for his dog, wondering when they would stop their charade. Instead of being protected from a painful experience, this boy was learning the art of manipulation and retaliation.

The question I ask parents who lie to protect their children is this: "Would you go to someone for support, knowing they have been dishonest with you?" The answer most parents give is, "Of course not. When we have concerns, we go to people who are honest with us."

Another concern is that when children become teenagers, their issues become more complicated. If parents are dishonest with their young children, they lose their influence when their children become teenagers.

*Recently, a parent told me a family secret, while
his five-year-old child was playing with a toy in front
of us. I said to the parent, "I think he knows." The
parent replied, "Ah, he did not hear that." To prove
my suspicion, with the parent's permissxion I asked
the child, "Do you know?" The child explained the
secret in his five-year-old language.*

Insights for the Mentoring Parent:

A parent's commitment to truth is a commitment to
managing the complexities of life with children.
Truthfulness creates a strong bond. Be honest with your
children.

Quality #3: Be All That You Can Be!

*Mentoring parents want their children to acquire
their unique talents.*

Mentoring parents strive to help their children acquire
three sets of skills that lead to their unique talents:

1. *Dependency* – Dependency is a helpful skill if used
   properly. It means relying temporarily on another person for support. After children recover from a painful
   event, they can renew their efforts to acquire their talents. For example, when children experience a loss, it
   is appropriate for them to be temporarily dependent on
   parents. As they recover from the loss, they will stop
   being dependent and return to their normal life.

   The key to dependency is to know when to stop
   using it. Over-dependency becomes a problem when
   children do not stop using dependency and refuse to

retake the reigns of their life. Over-dependency stops children from acquiring their skills, talents and self-reliance. Mentoring parents help their children learn how to use dependency.

2. *Mutual relationships* – A mutual relationship develops when sharing, concern, and agreement between people matures. For example, when spouses consider and negotiate with each other before making decisions, a solid mutual relationship develops. Mutual relationships occur in classrooms when children take turns, stand in line together, and help one another with assignments. Mutual relationships help relationships thrive and grow, and offer children support to acquire their special skills and talents.

3. *Self-Reliance* – Self-reliance is having confidence in one's own judgment and acting on that judgment. There are times in every person's life when you've got to handle a problem yourself. Children are no different. They need confidence to become self-reliant, so they can handle any circumstance. When mentoring parents model self-reliance, they teach their children how to manage life.

Overindulgent children usually become over-dependent and unable to have mutual relationships and self-reliance. In other words, they know how to get parents to give them what they want, but they do not know how to share, show concern, or reach agreement with others. Nor do they learn how to stand on their own two feet. Without these skills, they cannot gain their unique talents or manage the complexities of life, because they are taught only to be over-dependent.

Mentoring parents teach their children how to be dependent, interdependent, and self-reliant. Consider these further thoughts about these three sets of skills:

Dependency:

Children instinctively cling to their parents when a sad event occurs. Mentoring parents help children heal by facing the truth of the sad event, experiencing the sad emotions, and discussing the sad event together.

Indulgent parents only offer children overindulgence, with the belief the overindulgence will magically erase their children's unhappiness. Unfortunately, overindulged children become over-dependent and expect their parents fix their problems with more overindulgence.

Mutual Relationship:

Mentoring parents teach children to consider how their behavior affects others so they show concern for others. This leads children to work well at school and in relationships. They take their turn, are less likely to interrupt, and have a sense of fairness for themselves and others.

Overindulgent parents teach their children to focus on themselves which leads them to believe they require special treatment. This causes overindulgent children to become demanding and obnoxious whenever they are around other people. They learn to think of themselves only, and have little concern for others.

Self-Reliance:

Children need to become self-reliant. For example, parents can help their children study for a test, but at some point their children have to take the test themselves. Parents can advise a teenager on handling a conflict with another teenager, but at some point the teenager needs to manage the conflict on his or her own. Mentoring parents explore options with their children so their children gain the confidence to make better choices and take the reigns of their lives.

Unlike overindulgent parents, mentoring parents rarely force their unmet goals and dreams onto their children. They realize that children who aim for their parents' unmet goals and dreams lose the opportunity to acquire their own dreams.

Mentoring parents continue to actively pursue their dreams throughout life. Watching parents strive toward goals and dreams is an excellent quality for children to model. Mentoring parents encourage their children to pursue their goals and dreams, and offer support as well as constructive criticism to encourage and promote their children's sense of accomplishment and self-reliance.

Rationalizations About Talents and Skills:

Some overindulgent parents believe their children have the same needs and dreams they had when they were children. So, they try to make their children happy by giving them what they wanted when they were children, but this results in giving children what the parents wanted and not what the child wants. This is like trying to put a three-prong plug into a two-prong outlet. Despite their best efforts, no real connection occurs.

Many overindulgent parents believe their children cannot attain self-reliance. So they stop their children from taking the risks necessary to become self-reliant. One 12-year-old child I counseled had a bully problem. Bullies usually isolate vulnerable children before they hurt them.

So, managing a bully demands self-reliance because no one is there to help.

This 12-year-old boy's mother thought it was unfair that this much larger bully was picking on her son. Instead of mentoring her child, she took the reigns. She marched her son to the bully's home, confronted his parents and threatened legal action if the bullying persisted. The bullying got worse, of course, because the bully used the boy's mother's visit as leverage for more hazing. Now the bully called her son a wimp, because he had to have his mommy help him.

This 12-year-old boy did not learn how to handle bullies. When he becomes an adult and his employer is not fair, he will not have his mother to confront his employer. He will not know what to do, because he was taught to have his mother handle it. He needs advice—and experience— on handling bullies now, so he can become self-reliant as an adult.

Insights for the Mentoring Parent:

Teach children how and when to use dependency, interdependency, and self-reliance. Children can be temporarily dependent when they have a sad event in life. But they need to learn how to stop being so dependent so they can get on with life. With these parent-mentoring skills, children have a climate to pursue their real talents. In Chapter 5, you will receive parenting techniques to help create these three sets of skills within children.

Quality #4: Unconditional Love

*Mentoring parents strive to offer children uncon-
ditional love, but mentoring parents do not
define unconditional love as children getting
and doing whatever they want. They also understand that unconditional love means allowing
children to experience the consequences of
their misbehavior. Mentoring parents realize
that consequences help children create self-
guidance.*

Mentoring parents do not confuse unconditional love
with permissiveness and a lack of discipline. They realize
their children need to experience the consequences for misbehavior.

*Sixteen-year-old Monte had a history of behavior
problems, but never a legal problem until he kicked
his friend's car. He was angry with his friend, so he
dented his car. I had helped his parents become less
overindulgent, so they knew he needed to face the full
consequences of his actions.*

*Monte's parents had received a disturbing phone
call from the parents of Monte's friend, who owned
the damaged car, to discuss pressing charges against
Monte. His overindulgent parents knew if charges
were not pressed, Monte would not receive the full
consequences for his misbehavior. That meant he
would not learn from his bad decision. If charges
were filed, Monte would enter the legal system, which
was frightening to Monte's parents. Nevertheless,
they agreed that charges were in order and that their
son should pay the consequences for his actions.*

Let your children experience the full consequences of their misbehavior. If you buffer your children from the consequences of their misbehavior, your children's behavior will get worse. Only buffer children from consequences when there is a serious risk of psychological or physical harm.

Mentoring parents teach their children to manage life within the rules of our society. When a child kicks another child, an indulgent parent makes excuses for the child or blames someone else. A mentoring parent considers it a self-centered act and disciplines the child by helping their children realize that having a great ability to kick is not an excuse for nasty behavior.

Rationalizations for Buffering Consequences:

"My children are so unique and special, they should not follow the same rules as everyone else." This rationalization leads children into a self-centered attitude. Mentoring parents understand that while they view their children as unique and talented, they require their children to follow the rules of school and home.

Many overindulgent parents believe that experiencing the consequences for their misbehavior will hurt their children's self-esteem. They fear their children will become unhappy and dissatisfied with their life if they have to face consequences of their actions.

Insights for the Mentoring Parent:

Children who never feel the discomfort of consequences for their misbehavior become self-centered, believing they can do anything and get away with it. They view their parents as a tool, designed to get them out of trouble.

To gain influence with children, predict what will happen to them if they continue to misbehave, whether or not they believe those predictions. When your predictions come true, you will become more credible to your children.

Quality #5: Normal Emotions Are Healthy Emotions

Mentoring parents realize that children need to feel and express normal emotions. Normal emotions are healthy emotions and have messages which contribute to children's self-guidance and self-reliance.

Normal emotions are emotions that fit a situation. If children experience a joyous event, the normal emotion would be joy. If they experience a loss, the normal emotions would be an array of grief emotions. If they experience a crisis, the normal emotions would be crisis reactions. If they had been victimized by violence, the normal emotions would be trauma reactions.

Children do not realize that all normal emotions exist for a reason. When children feel uncomfortable emotions, they need a mentoring parent to attach good thinking to normal but uncomfortable emotions. This stops children from attaching cognitive distortions to their normal emotions.

If children do not understand their normal emotions, they have a natural tendency to attach distorted thinking to them. So, when children feel the normal emotions of grief, they may think, "What's wrong with me?" A mentoring parent can attach good thinking to children's grief emotions by assuring them that these uncomfortable emotions are normal. When children experience normal emotions that are pleasant or unpleasant, mentoring parents can teach children valuable lessons.

Twelve-year-old Jeremy and his uncle had great fun together on his uncle's ranch. Jeremy spent every weekend with his uncle and he dearly loved his uncle. When his uncle died in a car accident, Jeremy was devastated.

His parents hated to see him suffer, and it was tempting for them to overindulge Jeremy in order to console him. However, they resisted this temptation. Instead, they told him they understood his anguish, and assured him that anguish was a natural emotion to feel when losing a loved one. They encouraged him to remember all the neat and wonderful gifts his uncle had given him, the time they spent together, the fun, support, memories, and affection. They told him that it was perfectly normal for him to feel anguish because he loved his uncle. They told Jeremy they felt the same anguish too.

Instead of trying to distract Jeremy with overindulgence, his mentoring parents taught Jeremy how to grieve. Jeremy bonded with his parents, because they understood and allowed him to grieve in his own way.

Because of his parents' guidance, Jeremy will be able to handle other difficult life experiences. He had parents who cared enough to provide the mentoring and direction he needed to build healthy emotions.

Rationalizations for Erasing Normal, but Uncomfortable Emotions:

Overindulgent parents believe they are acting as caring parents when they protect their children from natural, but uncomfortable emotions. They believe they can relieve children's emotional pain with the quick-fix happiness of overindulgence. Some overindulgent parents believe that if they alter reality, they can stop their children from feeling painful emotions. So, overindulgent parents tell children Grandpa is sleeping when Grandpa is dead. They may tell their children the family dog is missing, instead of the truth that their dog is dead.

Insights for the Mentoring Parent:

Children need mentoring parents who will help them face reality together, and teach them the meaning of uncomfortable emotions. Truth, combined with good thinking, helps children understand their natural emotions and helps them learn to manage life.

Children need important instruction about their emotions. Get a children's dictionary and look up the words describing the various emotions. A children's dictionary has a simple way of describing emotions that children will understand. When you see your children feeling embarrassment, grief reactions, or any other uncomfortable emotions, tell your children the name of these emotions and why they exist. Children need to know that their emotions are natural and normal.

Quality #6: "Wants" vs. "Needs"

Mentoring parents know the difference between children's "needs" and children's "wants."

Loving parents feel a strong need to fulfill their children's needs (safeguarding their children's life, offering love, giving affection), but they feel no strong need to fulfill their children's "wants for luxuries" (expensive activities, colleges, investments, toys, cars). As I mentioned earlier, children's "want for luxuries" has nothing to do with parental love or with the quality of family relationships. Mentoring parents can express love, without giving expensive luxury items to their children. They can show love:

- ◆ with hugs and loving touch.
- ◆ with a natural interest and loving investment of time with their children.
- ◆ by helping children learn their talents and skills.
- ◆ by gradually offering freedom to children as they become older and more responsible.
- ◆ by inviting them to believe in God.
- ◆ by giving them good thinking when they have uncomfortable emotions.
- ◆ by practicing the qualities of a mentoring parent.
- ◆ by always being a genuine and honest parent.
- ◆ by advising children about their flaws.

Our generation of parents is having the greatest difficulty with overindulging children with wants (expensive activities and luxuries), while ignoring children's needs (especially the depth of instruction about life that mentoring parents can offer). To reduce excessive materialism, I have a suggestion that will help parents create a better relationship with their children. Give children gifts on birthdays and holidays only! This is a difficult instruction for overindulgent parents to fulfill, but a worthy one. When parents limit giving their children excessive material possessions, it forces parents to connect with their children beyond the "marketing" definition of happiness. Consider the following story:

Two months after Christmas, Allen's son was doing his usual begging and whining for a new toy, and was so emotionally upset that he looked like he would burst if he did not get a new toy. Allen considered buying his son the toy, but instead asked his son what his favorite Christmas present was. His son could not remember any of the gifts he had received for Christmas.

That is how meaningless excess is. If materialism is the basis of a parent-child relationship, the relationship is just as meaningless. Mentoring parents realize materialism is pricey, but love is priceless.

Mentoring parents realize that overindulgence spoils children and damages family bonding. When parents overindulge their children, they tie their worth as parents to their purse strings. Children view their parents as wonderful when they indulge, and less than wonderful when they do not indulge, in effect saying, "You are worthy when you give me things, and unworthy when you do not." Mentoring parents refuse to overindulge their children because they realize they do not need overindulgence to have loving relationships with their children.

Rationalizations for Giving Too Much:

Many overindulgent parents believe their children's demands for the best luxuries reflect the high standards of their children's excellent self-esteem. Recently, I was working with a girl who refused to go to school unless she was wearing designer clothes. Her parents believed that her demand for the best designer clothes was a reflection of her high self-esteem. In reality, she needed the designer clothes to feel good about herself, because her self-esteem was so low.

Insights for the Mentoring Parent:

Have a firm understanding of the differences between "demands" and "wants."

Demands – A demand is a want for luxury items that are extras (toys, expensive electronics, televisions in bedrooms, cars). Children do not need these items to have good relationships with parents. Luxury items are helpful if children learn how to earn the luxuries they want in life. Teach your children how to work and save money to get luxuries. As I mentioned previously, my best suggestion is that parents only give luxury items to their children for birthdays and holidays.

Children can also demand freedoms they are not ready to handle. For example, dating at a young age, deciding on where to spend the family money, or deciding whether or not they should attend church—are all common decision points overindulged children want to control.

Needs – A need is something that is necessary for preserving life and relationships. To survive, children need housing, water, food, cleanliness, and heat in the winter. For relationships, children need affection, affiliation, encouragement, safety, trust, authenticity from parents, honesty, mentoring and more.

Overindulgent parents erroneously believe that luxuries for children are necessary. They believe that the greater the number of luxury items their children have, the greater their children's self-esteem. More importantly, overindulgent parents view excessive materialism as a statement of their love. The more they give, the more they believe they are showing their love. Mentoring parents realize that overindulgence does not elevate self-esteem. It creates dependency, entitlement, and anger.

Quality #7: The Past, Present, and Future

The past does not control mentoring parents because they understand how the past influences the present and the future.

The field of psychology has missed an important opportunity in the last twenty years. When treating adults with childhood issues, many mental health clinicians of the 1980s focused on rehashing their adult clients' past and ignored addressing their present concerns or planning for their future.

I believe some past-oriented clinicians directed adult clients into an aimless and self-centered focus on their unmet childhood needs, which prompted them to view themselves as victims of their childhood when they were not victims at all.

Instead of an obsession with the past, parents need to review their past (not obsess about it), and consider its impact on their present life and future. In other words, they should consider this question: "How will reflecting on the past create a better life now and in the future?"

Mentoring parents do not obsess about the past nor do they define themselves as victims, because they have a clear direction in their lives. This makes them attractive leaders that children will naturally want to follow. Mentoring parents appreciate the good experiences from their past, learning from it instead of becoming victims.

Debra was truly abused as a child. Her abusive childhood interfered with her parenting. She had not become the parent she wanted to be for her children. Because of her past abuse, she was so overprotective that she stopped her children from having a normal life. She would not allow her children to enjoy the

*usual activities and events associated with childhood.
She realized she was overprotective, but she could not
control it. Concerned for her ability as a parent, she
sought counseling to review her past.*

*One of her goals was to release herself from her
over-protectiveness, so she could be a better parent.
As she reviewed her abusive past, she remembered
that as a child she grieved the loss of having normal
childhood experiences. She remembered not having
the freedom to invite friends for overnights and parties, and recalled how the abuse kept her away from
many normal activities with her friends.*

*Her counselor helped her realize that her over-
protectiveness was offering the same severe
limitations to her children. Debra became a mentoring parent the day she used this insight to lower her
over-protectiveness and allow her children to participate in normal activities.*

*Whenever family problems occurred, Dennis' par-
ents lied to him. They believed they were protecting
him. As a child, instead of hearing that a relative died,
the relative just disappeared from Dennis' life with no
explanation. When there were obvious stresses in his
parents' relationship, his parents refused to talk about
them. All of this protectiveness made Dennis feel iso-
lated from his parents.*

*When Dennis became a parent, he withheld infor-
mation from his children. Of course, when children
feel family tensions and have no explanation, they
often conjure up feelings of guilt and shame. Through
counseling, Dennis was able to recall his childhood*

insecurities and realized he created the same feelings of confusion, guilt, and shame in his children. He rehearsed being more open and honest with his children. His children immediately responded positively—and thankfully—to his openness. Dennis was well on his way toward becoming a mentoring parent.

In the accounts above, both Debra and Dennis reviewed their past, changed their present life, and looked forward to a brighter future as mentoring parents. Instead of obsessing about past abuses or tensions, they gained insights into their old issues, which allowed them to create positive changes in their lives and the lives of their children. Both parents could have chosen to wallow in anger over their imperfect childhoods, but they realized that would make them lousy parents. Instead, they chose to create good relationships with their children.

Rationalizations for Obsessing About the Past:

Some parents have real abuse issues in their childhood. Others exaggerate their abuse. Whether the abuse was real or exaggerated, what parents do with these issues is important. Many times parents believe the issues of the past justify their anger. They believe that it was unfair that they had abusive childhoods, and they obsess about the unfairness of the world. This affects how they adjust to life and keeps them stuck in the past.

Insights for the Mentoring Parent:

If you experienced abuse as a child, you need to confront it and deal with it. There is no doubt that childhood abuse has a devastating effect when abused children become parents. When parents have abusive childhood issues to

115

work through, one goal of counseling is to gain good parenting skills. Parents with abusive childhoods typically did not have strong models for good parenting. But they know what they did not get from abusive parents, and this insight helps parents who were abused become better parents. For example, abused parents know they did not get safety as children, so they learn to teach their children how to feel safe. They know they did not get affection, so they learn how to show affection and compassion with their children.

Although their parents abused them as children, they probably had other adults in their childhood who modeled good parenting. They had favorite teachers, uncles and aunts, or a loving grandparent who knew how to bond with children. Remembering that they had other wonderful adults in their childhood gives them good examples to emulate with their children.

If you experienced a really abusive childhood, consider counseling, especially counseling that helps transform old issues into good qualities you can use today.

Quality #8: Realistic Understanding Of Strengths and Limits

Mentoring parents realize that having strengths and limits is a normal human condition. They have a realistic appraisal of their own personal strengths and limits, and give their own children a realistic and hopeful appraisal of their strengths and limits as well.

Mentoring parents are usually humble and modest. They do not brag, but they can correctly describe their accomplishments and failures. When parents know their strengths and limits, they never exaggerate their talents or their children's talents. In fact, they know that exaggeration will lead to distorted labels which harm children.

Consider this distorted label: How many parents do you know who believe they have a gifted child? Research says that only 3% of the population is gifted, but I believe every third parent I talk to has a gifted child! Often they have a bright child, not a gifted child. But the label "gifted" is a distorted label if it is applied to a non-gifted child. Before entering school many overindulged children believe they are gifted. What a humiliating experience it must be for children to learn publicly that they are not gifted.

Mentoring parents are able to help their children honor their individuality without distorted labels such as "gifted." They spend quality time with their children, helping them understand their strengths and limits. They honestly praise the strengths of their children and realistically encourage them to improve their talents and skills.

Joey was never going to be a mathematician, since he could not decipher even the easiest math problems. His mother was a practical mentor who was honest with Joey. She would often tell him stories of great people in history who had limits: Einstein with his learning disability; Churchill with his childhood behavior problems; and Roosevelt with his physical disability. Joey's mother described these people as having great talents, but also great limits. She would often say to him, "Our wonderful talents make us feel good about ourselves, and our limits keep us humble."

Being a realist, she reminded Joey of his advanced ability to read. She also gave him a calculator and affectionately said, "You're going to need this." The gift she offered Joey was the realistic opportunity to

*honor his talents and accept his limits. But perhaps
her greatest gift was accepting Joey as he was.*

Rationalizations for Distorting Strengths and Limits:

Mentoring parents, like Joey's mother, are accepting of
others, but they encourage others to progress and not remain
stuck within their limits. They continually assess their children's strengths and limits and offer positive and productive
advice.

When overindulgent parents see their children as perfect, they ignore the real limits of their children and never
give their children instruction on how to fix their limits.
Their prevailing thought is, "If my child is perfect, there are
no limits to correct." This distorted view stops parents from
realizing the real limits of their children. It removes the first
step of self-improvement—identifying children's limits.
When overindulgent parents pamper their children, their
children never hear any real constructive criticisms until
they go to school. This, of course, puts these children at a
severe academic disadvantage.

Insights for the Mentoring Parent:

Mentoring parents accept their children as individuals,
but they strive to include a realistic look at their strengths
and limits. Like Joey's mother, mentoring parents promote
their children's natural talents and strive to give them real
solutions to compensate for their limits. When mentoring
parents teach their children how to manage their limits, they
are saying, "I will lovingly teach you to compensate for or
work toward overcoming your limits, and you can use this
knowledge. It is a gift for you." When this happens, children
learn to accept their limits so they can strengthen their talents. These children are ready to communicate with adults,

such as teachers, counselors, principals, police officers, and employers, on an adult level because they've developed their interpersonal skills along with their particular talents and abilities.

Recall someone in your life who cared enough to be honest with you, even with sensitive issues. This was a real mentor! Mentoring parents always offer loving statements when they mention a child's limitation. Make a list of the strengths and limits of your children. Plan and rehearse how to honestly praise your children's strengths as well as encourage them to off-set their limitations.

Quality#9: Respect For All

Mentoring parents promote respect for all groups.

Mentoring parents are respectful to all groups of people and encourage their children to do the same. This does not mean that mentoring parents agree with everyone and every lifestyle. They have various opinions based on their values and views about controversial topics. Mentoring parents can passionately discuss, debate, and disagree about hot controversial topics (such as homosexuality, abortion, right to die), but still offer respect and appreciation for those who disagree with them.

Mentoring parents express their opinions, but they refrain from one-upmanship, revenge, or retaliation, and don't become obnoxious with those who disagree with them. They are passionate about their opinions, but they feel no need to force opinions onto others. They are usually very influential with their children because they teach them how to develop their own opinions rather than forcing children to agree with them.

Tom was politically conservative and his college daughter was ultraliberal. Because they did not agree on any of the hot political issues, they had heated but respectful discussions on abortion, right to die, environmental issues, and more—but never got angry at each other. Tom always allowed his daughter the freedom to explore many ideas and opinions. He did not feel threatened by her contrary views. When he considered his boyhood, he recalled having many of the same ideas as his daughter and how important those ideas were to him. He realized his daughter was entitled to her views, and that he would respect those views.

Marilyn loved both of her children equally, but one of her sons was more difficult and required more attention, overseeing, and discipline. Because she could express love and affection equally, both of her children felt they were loved, and recognized one might receive more attention from time-to-time than the other.

Mentoring parents appreciate people's differences in culture and background. They see all people as equal, and teach their children to accept others. They also love their children equally and teach them to take care of others. However, they realize that loving their children equally does not mean they raise their children the same. Children are unique and deserve the right to be raised according to their uniqueness.

Rationalizations for Not Respecting Others:

Overindulgent parents see their children as superior to others, and competitively compare and contrast them with others. They try to prove their children's superiority, which means that they ignore their children's limits and skill deficiencies. They also believe there is no need to correct their children, because they think their children are perfect. They expect others (such as teachers, counselors, principals) to grant their children special privileges.

Insights for the Mentoring Parent:

Give your children the freedom to be different, and to offer their ideas and opinions. Sanctioning this free exchange helps children develop their individuality and social skills. As children mature, they will remember your openness to their ideas and advice. It is amazing to see children become adults and accept their parents' ideas about how to live life. But this only happens with a free exchange of ideas.

It is a great idea to expose children to other cultures. This helps children learn there are culture-specific reasons people from different countries act in different ways. This creates children who are tolerant of others, and who can appreciate the diversity other cultures offer.

Quality #10: Values

Mentoring parents have well-defined values and practice their values daily.

Mentoring parents carry their values with them everywhere they go. Their values are constant and stable. They do not separate their "self" from their behavior, and their behavior reflects their values. So, parents who practice their values can go anywhere (church, casino, tavern, park, work, and home) and they act with integrity. Couples who exercise good basic values trust their partners because they have good moral values, ethics, and loyalty to the marital relationship. Mentoring parents know that having healthy values makes life less complicated for them and their loved ones. For example, if parents are loyal to each other, they offer a firm foundation for each person in their family to flourish. If one parent is disloyal, the entire family is at risk.

Children can predict their parents' reactions when complications in life occur, because mentoring parents are stable and consistent. Parents' stability and consistency are especially important since children learn most of their values by watching their parents. When parents are inconsistent with their values, children become confused. When parents have stable values, their children feel more secure. For example, if both parents are honest, children feel stable; if one parent is dishonest, however, children become confused and feel insecure.

Mentoring parents realize their behavior is a reflection of their values, although our culture seems to be losing this idea. Mentoring parents value taking responsibility for their actions and make no excuses. Their children also take responsibility for their actions, which includes the consequences for their misbehavior.

Mentoring parents have a firm commitment to basic values (safety, honesty, authenticity), which are essential for family members. They also have a deep commitment toward values which create individual differences and define each family member's personality. Mentoring parents understand that values are foundational for healthy families, that they have a purpose, and allow children to feel stable and secure in their relationship with their parents.

Rationalizations for a Lack of Basic Values:

"You cannot tell me my values," is a comment that many adults and children make today. They believe it is their individual right to pick their values. However, without the basic values of safety, trust, fidelity, affiliation, acceptance, honesty, and fairness, it is impossible to have good relationships with others. Families without a core set of values have shaky foundations. Their children become so concerned about the lack of values that they cannot function adequately. Overindulgent parents believe their children have the necessary values, whether they do or not. This sounds like unconditional love, but it is not. Certain behaviors do not reflect the accompanying values which make them believable or warranted. Overindulgent parents overlook their children's misbehavior and lack of values, thinking, "This is a good child with a bad behavior." But when does a liar become a liar? When does a thief become a thief? Whether we like it or not, our culture labels people who lie and steal. When parents overlook their children's misbehavior, they also may be separating children from the emotional responsibilities of their misbehavior.

Insights for the Mentoring Parent:

Feel free to express your values, but advise children to express their values in such a manner that they are not stomping on the values of others. Help them feel comfortable with making their beliefs known to their children and a willingness to consider their children's ideas. Remember that your children's ideas are changing, that they are in motion and not solidified. Give your children the safety and freedom to develop their ideas with you.

SUMMARY

You now have the overindulgent parenting principles and the qualities of the mentoring parent. In the next chapter, let's use these overindulgent parenting principles to analyze your responses to your children's misbehavior. Then, we will use the qualities of the mentoring parent to help you effectively change your parenting to become a mentoring parent.

- CHAPTER 4 -

The Mystery of Children's Misbehavior—Solved

All children misbehave. As you know, parental reactions to children's misbehavior are critical. One significant problem for overindulgent parents is that they view their children's misbehavior too positively, which typically leads overindulgent parents to under-react to their children's misbehavior. This practice usually increases the misbehavior.

In this chapter, you will learn the purpose of common misbehaviors that all children perform. It will show you how to replace overindulgent parenting beliefs with the qualities of the mentoring parent. As we discuss each common behavior problem, we also will discuss which of the overindulgent parenting beliefs encourage these misbehaviors. Then, I will give suggestions for you to correct your children's misbehaviors using the qualities of the mentoring parent.

Back-Talk

The Purpose of Back-Talk:

Children who back-talk want power. Back-talk is a verbal punch children use to control others. Since they are nasty when back-talking, they are also seeking revenge. Overindulgent parents have a pattern of giving in to back-talking children, which gives them too much power. When children realize this, they grab for more power by using more back-talk.

Some children use back-talk to push their parents' buttons, which ignites their parents into an explosive tirade. When this happens overindulgent parents feel guilty after their tirade. The combination of tirade and guilt leads overindulgent parents to give in even more to their children. When overindulgent parents give in, they feel relieved from their guilt for getting angry at their children. This pattern (children back-talking and parents raging and giving in) becomes ingrained in dysfunctional families.

Always consider which of the overindulgent parenting beliefs you may be using. All children will occasionally back-talk, but back-talking becomes severe when overindulgent parents do not correct it. Consider these overindulgent parenting beliefs which increase children's back-talk.

Indulgent Parenting Beliefs That Encourage Back-Talking:

Whatever You Want!: Indulgent parents believe that unconditional love means children should receive and do whatever they want.

Many overindulgent parents are loving parents who want their children to have all possible advantages and work to make them available to their children. Unfortunately, they believe letting their children back-talk is one of the rights their children should have. They believe that if their children want to back-talk, it is fine, so overindulgent parents promote the belief, "Do whatever you want!"

This unrestrained back-talk travels into classrooms. Back-talking children who start back-talking with parents, generally back-talk teachers, school principals, and other adults in positions of authority. When children spread their back-talking into the classroom, it complicates their school experience and prevents them from building mutual relationships with classmates and teachers.

Shield from Consequences: Indulgent parents shield their children from the consequences of their children's actions, as well as the complications of life.

Overindulgent parents pamper their back-talking children by buffering them from the consequences of their misbehavior. Consequences are uncomfortable, so overindulgent parents stop their discomforting effects by being over-permissive with their children. Their overindulged children expect this same pampering from others. In other words, since their parents did not give them consequences for back-talking, these children do not expect consequences from other adults.

Juanita back-talked all authority figures and she enjoyed it. Back-talking made her feel powerful and in control of every interaction. She back-talked her parents, teachers, principal, and any other authority figure she believed needed to suffer her wrath. However, when she back-talked her high school principal, her principal disciplined her with a detention. When she back-talked her high school principal again, the principal gave her Saturday School (a deeper form of detention from 7:00am to 11:00 a.m. Saturday morning). When she back-talked her principal a third time, the principal suspended her from school for three days.

Juanita believed that when she back-talked, she was in charge. She refused to accept that back-talking was helping her lose control of her life. Her back-talking got her the attention of her school principal, who dictated real consequences (detentions, Saturday school, and suspension). Juanita's mother needed to teach Juanita that her back-talking was creating problems for her. Instead, her overindulgent mother attempted to stop the principal's discipline. She worked hard to shield her daughter from the consequences that she earned because of her obstinacy.

I Will Correct My Parents' Mistakes: Indulgent parents believe that their parents raised them improperly, so they long to correct their own parents' mistakes by becoming perfect parents.

When some overindulgent parents were children, their parents restricted their freedom to speak by strictly enforcing the adage "children are to be seen and not heard." Some parents, who grew up in this strict environment, try to correct their parents' mistake by going to the other extreme. They give their children complete freedom to speak. Unfortunately, these parents become too permissive and allow their children to back-talk by advancing the belief, "I will correct my parents' mistakes by giving my child complete freedom!" In reality, they are creating a whole new set of mistakes.

A Mentoring Parent's Management of Children's Back-Talk:

Once you discover which of the overindulgent parenting beliefs you are using, you can replace overindulgent beliefs by using the qualities of the mentoring parent. Consider the following ideas and suggestions to mentor your children when they back-talk. Notice that the suggestions which reflect the qualities of the mentoring parent are in bold highlight:

- Mentoring parents realize they can **unconditionally love** their children, while **teaching limits** to them. Mentoring parents help children realize there is a point where self-expression becomes harmful to others, and back-talk crosses that line.

  In fact, when children back-talk they create conditional love. Many children use back-talk to get what they want so they can create over-permissive parents who buy into the child's philosophy that says, "When you give me what I want, you will be a good parent and I will stop back-talking—for a while."

  It is important for you to stop your children from back-talking. Ignoring children's back-talk is one technique, but it varies in its effectiveness. It is generally ineffective, because other children may encourage the back-taking child.

Another technique is to make children's back-talk ineffective. When children back-talk, they usually want something. Mentoring parents **never give back-talking children what they want.** What they want usually falls into three categories: toys, power, and activities.

If children's back-talking persists, confront your back-talking children by explaining the tactics they are using. "You are back-talking to get this toy, and you will never get it by back-talking." Then stick to this statement.

You can teach your children to get what they want. As a rule of thumb, the most suitable means for children getting what they want is **work, hard work.** Your children should work for what they want, because work is a healthy means for children getting what they want, and a great replacement for destructive back-talk and overindulgence.

- ◆ Back-talk gets children in trouble with school principals and teachers. If you tried to correct your children's back-talk, and children continue, allow your children to suffer the **full consequences** of their back-talk. If your child back-talks to the football coach and the coach kicks your child off the team, do not to rescue your child. Instead, **predict** for your child that these consequences will occur well before they actually happen. When your predictions come true, your child will see you as a mentor and a powerful force in changing their behavior and attitude. Mentoring parents do considerable predicting for their children.

    Prediction also keeps children from inflating their self-esteem, believing they know more than their parents. Parents' predictions keep children humble, which is a good quality that needs more practice.

- **The past does not control mentoring parents.** Mentoring parents will not let their own parent's strict parenting style hurt the parenting of their own children by being too permissive. If you have old issues that affect your current life, fix those old issues—even if it requires counseling. Mentoring parents will not allow old wounds to hurt the parenting of their children. They will get counseling if necessary, to **change old wounds into useful parenting tools.**

- Mentoring parents have **respect for all people.** They realize that back-talk is disrespectful, and advise their children to make amends to anyone they have disrespected.

Sulking, Nagging and Whining

The Purpose of Sulking, Nagging, and Whining:

Most overindulgent parents have caring hearts and will do anything to stop their children's sulking—and their children know it. When a child's lip sticks out in a pouting fashion, he or she is sulking. Sulking is a manipulative tool children used to gain attention, special activities, and toys. Sulking is a child's body language screaming, "Make me happy again, by giving me what I want!"

Children use nagging and whining to put pressure on parents to get them to give in to their demands. The strategy is that nagging and whining will grate on a parent's nerves or push guilt buttons(which they do) until the parent gives in. Children's nagging and whining increase because they know these behaviors pay off. But they never know when the payoff will happen because the payoffs are like winning a jackpot or a lottery.

Parents who give in to their children's sulking, nagging, and whining employ one or a combination of the following overindulgent parenting beliefs:

Constant Happiness: Indulgent parents believe that they can create good self-esteem in their children if their children are constantly happy.

Overindulged children often give their parents this message: "Make me happy by giving me the best, so I can be the best." Many parents believe this idea.

The biggest and best sulker I ever met in my career was a 17-year-old hockey player. This boy loved hockey, but his skills were not strong enough for him to become a professional hockey player. He believed that to become a better hockey player, he needed the "best" equipment. Unfortunately, his parents bought into this belief, thinking that the best equipment would make him happy and increase his self-esteem.

Even though he was 17 years old, he never had a job. Instead of working to get the best hockey equipment, the 6' 7" 250-pound teenager would stick out his big lip and sulk and whine to his parents. They believed the only way to make him happy was to buy him the best hockey equipment.

I suggested to his parents that their son needed to get a part-time job to help pay for his hockey equipment. When he heard my suggestion, the boy looked at his parents and stuck out his lip, whining, "He wants me to work at some place like a Wal-Mart!" The cou-

ple looked at their son with sympathetic eyes and his mother teared up. Then they looked at me as if I were an ogre!

Overindulgent parents believe that normal expectations (such as work) are abnormal for their "special" children. Instead of working, their children learn to sulk, nag, and whine. Unfortunately, there is an undercurrent of permissiveness in this culture that reinforces whining and self-indulgence. Our "pop culture" heavily rewards its heroes for their whining and self-indulgence. Consider the examples of sports and entertainment personalities who do whatever they want, no matter who it hurts, because they think they are "special." Children see their whininess and self-indulgence continually rewarded with money, movie contracts, and endorsements. It seems misguided celebrities can get away with anything and continue their professional lives (or should I say lies) almost without interruption.

This idiocy of our "pop culture" is tough competition for parents who try to convince their children that misbehavior does not pay off. What children do not realize is that special privileges for the arrogant and uncouth celebrities of this world are rare. Children, especially young and impressionable children, need parents to teach them that important fact.

Wishy-Washy Decisions: Indulgent parents have difficulty with firm decisions and usually make wishy-washy decision when they do.

Many parents believe that when children sulk and whine, they should negotiate with them to help them feel they are part of the decision-making process. There is a fundamental problem that makes negotiating with nagging and whining children nearly impossible. When parents negotiate, their goal is to achieve fairness for both parties. Nagging and whining children are immature and they only want to win!

Negotiation is an excellent technique with most teenagers, when they are mature enough to be fair with negotiations, but it does not work with nagging, whining, and immature children who want to win. When parents give in to nagging and whining children, parents become wishy-washy!

Too Trusting: Indulgent parents are too trusting.

When parents are too trusting, they become gullible. When children sulk, their pain and sadness are not real. Overindulgent parents gullibly react to their children's best portrayal of pain and sadness, as if these portrayals were real emotions. When parents gullibly believe their children's fake emotions are real, power transfers from parents to children. Sulking children try to make parents feel guilty so they give in.

One seven-year-old boy, whose mother I eventually trained as a mentoring parent, was an expert at creating so much guilt within his mother that he influenced her decisions. When he was in a department store with her, he would beg for a new toy. Initially, his mother would refuse to buy it. When she finally gave in, the boy said, "I don't want it." Despite her pleas for him to reconsider, he refused. She felt even more guilt. This boy was training his mother to say "Yes" the first time he asked.

A Mentoring Parent's Management of Children's Sulking, Nagging, and Whining

Once you discover which of the overindulgent parenting beliefs you are using, you can replace those distorted beliefs by reviewing the qualities of the mentoring parent. Consider the following ideas and suggestions to mentor your sulking, nagging, and whiney offspring. As before, the suggestions that reflect the qualities of the mentoring parent are in bold highlight:

◆ Mentoring parents are immune to their children's sulking, nagging, and whining. They know that children's **sulking, nagging, and whining are not real emotions,** but manipulative games to get what they want.

Ignore children's attempts to manipulate with sulking, nagging, and whining. If you respond— even once—to children's fake emotions, their sulking, nagging, and whining will dramatically increase. To help children reduce sulking, nagging, and whining you do not have to buy them anything, which is often the purpose of sulking, nagging, and whining. If children ask for special toys or activities when they are upset, your children are manipulating you. **Love and affection soothe real emotional pain,** but buying is not a requirement.

◆ Mentoring parents have a **heartfelt commitment to truth and reality.** When children sulk, nag, and whine, truthfully tell children that they are faking emotions to get what they want. Tell your children that they will never get what they want when they sulk, nag, and whine. Redirect children to work for what they want by telling children, "I will show you

135

how you can earn what you want, but I am not giving it to you." This redirection toward work teaches children that they can gain empowerment by working. On the other hand, giving in to them teaches them to be dependent. Mentoring parents want their children to receive all the wonderful experiences in life, but they want their children to earn what they get.

When parents teach their children to work, they are also teaching their children to save money, learn to be responsible, plan their finances, preserve their belongings, fulfill commitments, and many more important skills. The overindulged child is only learning to be dependent and to enjoy life's indulgences.

Crying

Purpose of Crying:

There are many sincere, as well as insincere, reasons for crying. The purpose of children's sincere crying can be a release of hurt, a release of frustration, an expression of helplessness, as well as an expression of happiness. For many children, the purpose of their crying is innocent, but how parents react to their children's tears could determine if their children's crying remains innocent.

There are two types of crying: sincere and insincere. Often, young children cry sincere tears when they are physically or emotionally hurt. Their crying is insincere when they have an agenda other than the sincere release of hurt. For example, when one of my children was small, his brother had a blanket that he wanted, so he cried at the top of his lungs. When his brother gave him the blanket, his crying stopped as quickly as if someone had turned off a faucet. Real emotional pain does not clear up that quickly.

Children use insincere crying to gain attention and manipulate others. Overindulgent parents react to their children's insincere crying as if it were sincere crying. When this occurs, children learn that their insincere crying works. So, they continue to pretend to be upset.

Many overindulgent parents, who are susceptible to children's insincere crying, often use one or more of the following overindulgent parenting beliefs:

Indulgent Parenting Principles That Encourage Insincere Crying:

Constant Happiness combined with Whatever You Want!: Indulgent parents believe that they can create good self-esteem in their children if their children are constantly happy, and they believe that unconditional love means children should receive whatever they want and do whatever they want.

To squelch unhappy emotions, overindulgent parents give their children quick-fix "marketing" happiness. In fact, quick-fix "marketing" happiness for children occurs in much of today's economy. For example, McDonald's sells *Happy Meals*. Christmas is one long commercial designed to pressure parents to get that one special toy they believe will create perfect happiness for their children. Most parents believe that to make their children happy, they must get their children to Disney World at least once. When they finally get to Disney World, their overstimulated children become ornery and cranky. This frustrates overindulgent parents who are trying to do everything to win their children's happiness.

With such pressure for happiness, crying is the enemy of the overindulgent parent because it says, "Your children are not happy, so they will not have good self-esteem!" These parents stop their children's crying by becoming even more overindulgent. They give their children whatever they want and let them do whatever they desire.

Shield from Consequences: Overindulgent parents shield their children from the consequences of their actions as well as the complications of life.

Overindulgent parents pamper their children by shielding them from the consequences of their misbehavior. Overindulged children use insincere crying to motivate parents to stop the consequences children earned.

When overindulgent parents excessively pamper their children, they are raising children who have no skills. Instead of learning to become self-reliant (which includes managing the consequences of your actions), pampered children learn to use insincere crying. This motivates their parents to continue pampering them by buffering them from consequences they earn.

A Mentoring Parent's Management of Children's Crying:

Once you discover which of the overindulgent beliefs you are using, you can review and use the appropriate qualities of the mentoring parent. Consider the following ideas and suggestions to mentor children when they insincerely cry. Again, the suggestions reflecting the qualities of the mentoring parent are in bold highlight:

- Mentoring parents who perceptively respond to children who sincerely cry create an **emotional bond.** They never offer toys and expensive activities to crying children because they realize these items do not sooth emotions.

- Mentoring parents debunk the cultural idea that parents should keep their children happy by buffering children from the complications of life. Mentoring parents realize there will always be complications in life that are emotionally sensitive and teach their children how to **manage emotionally sensitive issues.**

- Mentoring parents **experience and express their natural and normal emotions.** When parents understand their own emotions, it is easier to mentor their children during emotional reactions. Understanding their own emotions also allows parents to recognize their children's insincere crying. The solution for children's insincere crying is not toys and expensive activities. Instead, it is more helpful for parents to caringly confront and truthfully tell their children that they are playing a manipulative game.

- Mentoring parents know that when their children engage in insincere crying, they either want their parents to overindulge them or they want them to stop the consequences for their misbehavior. Mentoring parents never give in and grant children what they want when children perform insincere crying. Redirect your children toward **work and self-reliance,** and teach them to **face the consequences of their actions.**

◆ Mentoring parents realize that childhood cannot be emotionally painless, because life is not emotionally painless. They know that children need to learn how to manage unhappy events in life and the associated uncomfortable emotions. The best parents can do is to allow children to express emotions with loved ones. Mentoring parents can offer children a **safe atmosphere to express their emotions.**

When overindulgent parents rush to buy their children out of uncomfortable emotions, they are teaching their children that it is not normal to feel these natural emotions. Hugs may be less expensive, but they are much more powerful. When children hurt, they need **love, affection, and guidance**—not stuff. When children suggest that a new toy or privilege would help heal their pain, it is tempting to try to buy children out of their uncomfortable emotions. Don't do it!

Natural emotions (including uncomfortable emotions) have a purpose which gives children important information. For example, if a child hurt another person, the child may feel the natural emotion of guilt. This is a good thing! Parents can **attach good thinking** to their child's emotion of guilt by suggesting that the child make amends. This relieves the child's guilt and teaches the child to manage emotions and mend relationships.

Overindulged children learn to not feel their natural emotions, because they are so distracted with expensive toys and excessive activities. Unfortunately, overindulgent parents do not mentor their children, and without mentoring, children do not learn to attach good thinking to their natural emotions and end up losing good self-guidance. This will complicate their relationships with loved ones, because self-guidance leads children to make amends when they have misbehaved, and making amends enhances mutual relationships.

Mentoring parents help their children by attaching **good thinking** to their natural emotions. Consider the following examples:

◆◆ When children feel appropriate guilt because they hurt someone, mentoring parents suggest that their children need to make amends to release their guilt.

◆◆ When children feel anguish because a loved one died, mentoring parents explain that anguish is a normal emotion that teaches children how much they cared for their lost loved one.

◆◆ When children feel embarrassed by their misbehavior, mentoring parents teach children that embarrassment is a signal that they need to change their misbehavior.

All three of the above emotions are uncomfortable. Mentoring parents do not mask these uncomfortable emotions with false happiness. Instead, they explain the purposes of each emotion and teach their children to manage these emotions by changing their behavior.

Teasing and Bullying

Purposes of Teasing and Bullying:

Like all people, children desire status. Unfortunately, some children try to achieve status by using the status rituals of teasing and bullying. For example, when children gain status by teasing and bullying others, children feel they have the upper hand. Sadly, this status is shallow and hollow, because no one wants to bond with these children.

Overindulgent parents view their children's teasing and bullying in a positive light. They mislabel their children's teasing and bullying as an expression of affection, strength, a positive personality characteristic, or assertiveness. Because overindulgent parents mislabel children's teasing and bullying, teasing and bullying continue and generally become destructive. They mislabel their children's teasing and bullying for one or a combination of the following overindulgent parenting principles.

Indulgent Parenting Principles That Encourage Teasing And Bullying:

Sting-Free Discipline: Overindulgent parents either offer no discipline or take the sting out of their discipline.

Since overindulgent parents mislabel their children's teasing and bullying as a positive characteristic, they see no reason to discipline their children.

One parent I counseled many years ago became frustrated with the father of a bullying child. He made many attempts to explain to the bully's father that his son's bullying was too extreme. The father mislabeled his son's bullying behavior with the phrase, "Boys will be boys," belittling the reality of the bullying as typical boy behavior.

With his "Boys will be boys" philosophy, his son's bullying will continue. This allows parents who are bullying advocates to say, "If I see no problem with my child, there is no problem that needs correction." These children will continue to bully without the guiding influence of a mentoring parent.

I Will Correct My Parents' Mistakes: Overindulgent parents believe that their parents raised them improperly and long to correct their own parents' mistakes by becoming perfect parents.

Many parents raised by strict parents want to give their children more freedom. They try to correct their parents' mistakes by offering their own children too much freedom. Unfortunately, they give their children permission to express themselves completely, which includes hurtful teasing and bullying of others.

A Mentoring Parent's Management of Children's Teasing and Bullying

Once you discover which of the overindulgent parenting principles you are using, you can review the qualities of the mentoring parent. Consider the following ideas and suggestions to help mentor children when they tease and bully. The suggestions that reflect the qualities of the mentoring parent will be in bold highlight:

◆ Mentoring parents can sort the weeds from the grass, to use a gardening expression. Mentoring parents **truthfully** define children's good behavior and misbehavior. When mentoring parents learn that their children are hurting others with teasing and bullying, they do not minimize the impact. Instead, they evaluate this information, the source of the information, and their children, before deciding if there are real concerns with excessive teasing and bullying.

Mentoring parents know their children, because they **spend quality time** with them. They know if there is any history of excessive teasing and bullying from their children. Unlike overindulgent parents, mentoring parents do not use blinders. They allow themselves to see their children's flaws, and they deal with **truth and reality,** not distorted thinking.

◆ Mentoring parents do not try to raise perfect children, because they know that is impossible. Mentoring parents know what to do when their children are not so perfect. Once parents determine that their children are teasing and bullying, they can become **proactive. Create consequences** for your children when they tease and bully. You can also allow your children to **experience the full consequences** that come with being a bully. This usually includes school discipline, as school authorities often discipline bullies.

Offer a wide-range response to your children's teasing and bullying by contacting many resources. For example, one mother organized a meeting with her child's teacher, principal, and school counselor to coordinate a plan of action. This resulted in all parties consistently disciplining her child when he bullied other children. That's proactive parenting! That's mentoring at its best!

Tantrums

The Purpose of Tantrums:

A tantrum is a child's "fit" that simply states "I want my way and I want it now!" Tantrums are universal in all cultures and designed to command an audience.

When my own children were younger, I recall one of my children lying on the floor in the living room, wailing his arms and legs on the carpet. My wife and I removed ourselves as his audience by going into the den. The tantrum suddenly stopped and we heard little footsteps trotting down the hall. He entered the room with dry eyes, lay on the floor and continued with his tantrum. My wife and I calmly talked, ignoring him as his tantrum continued. Finally he quit, since his tantrum was not working.

At one of my parenting seminars, I talked with a mother who told me the traditional story (with a new twist) of her 5-year-old son, who wanted a treat at the grocery store. He spread out belly down in the middle of an aisle and started kicking and screaming. She lay down next to him and did the same. He was so embarrassed he ran and hid so people would not see him with her. That is a daring parent! He did not expect her reaction and he never performed another tantrum in a grocery store.

Our culture has become incredibly materialistic. When a child performs a tantrum in a store, it is easier for parents to give children what they want, hoping to stop the tantrum. Buying something to stop the tantrum might stop that one tantrum, but it will increase tantrums in the future.

To understand the mind-set of overindulgent parents who pay off their tantrum-ridden children, consider the following overindulgent parenting principles.

Indulgent Parenting Principles That Encourage Tantrums:

Whatever You Want! Overindulgent parents believe that unconditional love means children should receive whatever they want and do whatever they want.

When children do not get everything they want, they become frustrated. Overindulgent parents try to eliminate their children's frustration with excessive overindulgence, but the road to genuine happiness demands that children learn skills. When parents give children everything they want, children have no need or drive to learn skills. They only refine one skill: the art of becoming dependent on their parents. They refine their dependency with the destructive tools of guilt trips, manipulation, excuses, tantrums, anger, intimidation, and a host of other misbehavior. Overindulgent children use tantrums to pressure parents into more and more overindulgence!

Ignore tantrums! You can lead your children to the foundational tools they need when they ask for money, luxuries, and expensive activities. Consider the following examples:

Example 1:
    Child: "I want some money."
    Parent: "What job are you going to do for it?"

Example 2:
> Teenager: "Can I borrow the car?"
> Parent: "You can borrow it, if you wash and wax it first."

Example 3:
> Child: "Can my friend stay overnight?"
> Parent: "Yes, if you spotlessly clean your room."

Example 4:
> Child: "I'm hungry!"
> Parent: "Let's make supper together and then do the dishes together."

Review your children's favorite demands which in the past have been quickly fulfilled. In advance, decide which jobs you are going to require when children make these demands. Parents often ask me, "Do we have to make them earn everything?" The answer is no, but most children are not earning much of anything. They need to learn to earn most of what they want.

Instead of overindulging children when they have a tantrum, create the expectation that children need to earn a major portion of what they get. This expectation of work is important, because this is how the real world works.

Overindulgent parents believe they are unconditionally loving their children when they overindulge them. Children's tantrums say to parents, "Give me what I want," which is a perfect fit for parents who have difficulty saying, "No." So, parents offer leniency and overindulgence when their children have a tantrum, believing they are offering unconditional love.

When overindulgent parents say "No," they feel that they are withholding love. They often feel so badly that they explain to their children their reasons for saying "No." There are times when children need an explanation, and there are times when parents should not have to explain to children. When children use tantrums to get what they want, parents should answer "No" with no explanation, and then redirect overly-demanding children toward work.

Some overindulgent parents do a good job saying "No" to children but then their "No" reduces its sting and becomes a "Maybe." Their "Maybe" eventually becomes a "Yes." Overindulged children are usually very persistent. Persistence is a commendable quality when attached to good and decent motives, but is harmful when attached to manipulation. When children attach persistence to manipulation by using tantrums, they will run their parents ragged.

Mentoring Parents' Management of Children's Tantrums

Once you discover which of the overindulgent parenting principles you are using, replace them by reviewing the qualities of the mentoring parent. Consider the following ideas and suggestions to mentor children when they have tantrums. The suggestions that reflect the qualities of the mentoring parent are in bold highlight:

- Mentoring parents offer no audience to children when they perform tantrums. It is best if parents offer **no response or an unexpected response** to their children's tantrums. This will stop children from manipulating parents with tantrums.

- Children use tantrums to push parents' buttons, so they can get a new toy or expensive activity. **Mentoring parents know their own buttons** and can feel when their children have pushed them. When they feel their buttons pushed, mentoring parents create a psychological wall by **slowly contemplating how they want to respond.** This contemplation stops mentoring parents from acting impulsively, and allows them to either ignore their children's button pushing or create unexpected responses.

Frustration is a feeling that occurs when children cannot get what they want. Frustration is an emotion parents can use to motivate children. Mentoring parents realize that when children become frustrated, children have two choices to relieve their frustration. They can either have a tantrum or consider a productive **plan of work.**

◆ Tantrums are children's expression saying that they do not know how to get what they want. Tantrums are signals to you that it is time to **teach children how to get what they want.** But, children need to use a different set of behaviors instead of tantrums. Teach children to ask for odd jobs, so they can earn what they want.

For example, I suggested to one parent that she assign her son five extra jobs throughout the week, which allowed him to have his friend stay for one overnight. I advised another parent that his daughter should accumulate points whenever she baby-sat her sister. Her points allowed her to have more telephone time to call friends during the weekend.

Remember, it is important to insure that children complete all work assignments before they can get what they want. Offer no advanced credit! Parents should never give their children privileges first with the promise of work later. When children wait, they learn to delay gratification until they earn it. This is the way it is for adults. You work first, then you buy later. If not, you accumulate debt.

Children may not realize there are other choices to get what they want. You can teach children to **earn what they want by working.** This helps children create the characteristics of empowerment, self-reliance, and good character.

Blaming and Creating Scapegoats

Purposes of Blaming and Scapegoating:

Occasional blaming of others is typical of all children. When children blame others, they usually are trying to avoid responsibility for a problem, or they want to avoid a discipline. A solution is to separate children who are blaming one another and place them in a time-out until one confesses.

When my children were younger they had "blaming-itis." A vase in the living room was broken and I asked, "Who broke the vase?" Both boys pointed firm fingers at each other, singing in harmony, "He did it!" Both were convincing, and it was hard to decide which boy was lying and which was truthful. I told one boy to sit in the den and the other to sit in our bedroom, so they could not talk to each other. I told them, "When the one who is lying tells me the truth, you can both come out of these rooms. Otherwise, you can both stay there all day."

No one spoke for the first hour, or the second hour. During the third hour, one son stuck his head outside the bedroom door and asked, "What's going to happen to the person who did it?" I offered no answer. He

*asked the same question several times. Again I offered
no answer. Then we heard a meek voice say, "I did it."
I disciplined the guilty child with additional time-out.
He also had to compensate his innocent brother by
making his bed for a week.*

Occasional blaming is not unusual with children. In its
most severe form, scapegoating can become a major family
problem. Whoever is the scapegoat is given unjust blame for
everything that goes wrong in their family. There are real
advantages to scapegoating. If there is a family of six and
one person is the scapegoat, the other five are off the hook.
If one person is the scapegoat, everyone else in the family
does not have to accept responsibility for any family problems. They just blame the scapegoat.

To understand the mind-set of parents who scapegoat,
let us review the overindulgent parents' principles that
encourage scapegoating.

Overindulgent Parenting Principles That Encourage Scapegoating:

*Sting-Free Discipline: Overindulgent parents
either offer no discipline or take the sting out of
their discipline.*

Overindulgent parents scapegoat others instead of disciplining their children. Without discipline, parents do not
give their children caring insight that accompanies good
discipline. So, their children continue to scapegoat others.
Children who scapegoat are saying, "If I blame you, I do not
have to admit to my own flaws." This distorted conclusion
allows children to believe that only other people have flaws.
Without parental guidance, they never correct this distorted
thought or their flaws.

I Will Correct My Parents' Mistakes: Overindulgent parents believe their parents raised them improperly and long to correct their own parents' mistakes by becoming perfect parents.

Parents who had unhappy childhoods may frequently blame their own parents. Parents may or may not have justified reasons for being angry with their own parents. If there is real reason for their anger, parents have no justified reason to wallow in their anger. Parents may have had bad experiences in childhood, but they should not allow those experiences to hurt their own children. When parents continue to blame (justified or not) their own parents, children will model their parents' excessive blaming behavior.

Mentoring parents do not ignore their justified anger toward their parents. Instead they work through their anger in counseling, with the goal of improving their current life and future.

Who Am I And Why Am I Here?: Overindulgent parents have inadequately developed identities which hinder their ability to help their children develop their identities. They do not know who they are or why they are here.

Some parents were scapegoats in their families when they were children. Since they were scapegoats, they never had an opportunity to create a real identity. As parents, they continue with their role as a scapegoat, taking the blame for their children's misbehavior. Coupled with being the scapegoat, they often have the distorted belief that if they take the blame, their children will feel better about themselves.

Unfortunately, when their children scapegoat others, they do not feel better about themselves. Instead, they try to keep a false "king-of-the-hill" status. Many overindulgent children with poor self-esteem constantly fear losing their status. So, they continually scapegoat others to maintain their status.

In her blended family, Beth worried about her "king-of-the-hill" status with her stepbrother and stepsister. To ensure her status, she sabotaged her step-siblings' efforts to please their parents. When they cleaned their bedrooms, she would sneak in and mess them up. Her parents praised Beth for keeping her room clean and disciplined her siblings for having a messy room.

Beth convinced her stepbrother that his sister was messing up his bedroom, which created conflict between them. Because she did not appear to be part of the conflict, she won even higher status with her parents. They believed she was behaving well, especially in comparison to her two step-siblings.

Her need for false status was so strong that she was becoming a mild form of a "Bad Seed." She was learning to play games to pit people against each other instead of building a cooperative spirit. She played many manipulative games to gain a false sense of status within her family.

A Mentoring Parent's Management of Children Blaming and Creating Scapegoats:

Once parents discover which of the overindulgent parenting principles they are using, they can replace them by reviewing the qualities of the mentoring parent. Consider the following ideas and suggestions to help you mentor your children when children blame and scapegoat. The suggestions that reflect the qualities of the mentoring parent will be in bold highlight:

- There is a healthy purpose for honest blaming. **Truthful** blame serves this important purpose: if a child misbehaves and accepts blame, the child is taking the first step toward being responsible and making amends. When dishonest blaming occurs, children try to scapegoat others. Mentoring parents make every attempt to discover the **truth** and discipline children who inappropriately blame others.

- The solution for children who try to create a false status by blaming others is genuine self-esteem founded on solid skills. When parents **invest in children** by teaching them how to live life to its fullest, there is little need for false status.

- Also, mentoring parents do not waste their life losing control of their anger and scapegoating their parents. When children model angry parents, it is easy for them to scapegoat their parents. If mentoring parents are angry toward their own parents, they are secure enough to enter counseling to resolve their anger. Mentoring parents **strive to enhance their talents.** They realize that unresolved anger can destroy this goal and interfere with their real purpose in life.

Scapegoating destroys children's basic values, such as safety, authenticity, honesty, and integrity. When parents stop their children from scapegoating others, they are preserving these basic values within their children.

Lying

The Purposes of Lying:

There are several types of lying, each having a definite purpose:

Exaggeration: Children often use exaggeration to inflate their self-esteem when they lack confidence. Children who exaggerate stories feel like a "gray child," which is a child who does not excel at anything and, therefore, receives little attention. Gray children try to gain attention by using colorful exaggerations. So, when children exaggerate stories, loved ones may offer the enthusiastic attention these children crave.

Distorting the Truth: Distorting the truth is a much more serious lie, because it requires children to be more deceptive. They often have hidden motives, such as setting up another child to take the blame for their misbehavior; denying the truth to get out of trouble; or avoiding an undesirable activity (homework, chores).

Distorting the truth forces children to continue to lie to keep the original lie believable. With this more advanced lying, children actively rehearse lying to others and become more accomplished liars.

Lying by Omission: When children lie by omission, children withhold important information from their parents. Lying of this nature is serious, especially if the truth is obvious. For example:

I counseled a frustrated mother whose 16-year-old son routinely lied by omission. She was waiting for an important phone call, but she needed to run an errand. She instructed her son that if the phone call occurred while she was gone, to take a message and

*to let the caller know she will call him right back. The
caller was her new boyfriend that her son did not like.*

*Her son was angry about the divorce and wanted
to punish his mother, so when the boyfriend called, he
said his mother would not be home until the next day.
When his mother came home, he intentionally did not
mention the phone call to his mother. When he was
later confronted with his omission, he lied again by
denying it. He said her boyfriend was trying to create
trouble. "Mom, who do you believe, him or me?" His
original lie required continued lying, and continued
lying requires a greater commitment to becoming an
accomplished liar.*

All children will occasionally lie, but when children are
committed to lying, parental intervention is important. Parents can increase their children's lying behavior if they use
any of the following overindulgent parenting principles.

*Overindulgent Parenting Principles That
Encourage Lying:*

*Shield from Consequences: Overindulgent par-
ents shield their children from the
consequences of their children's actions as well
as the complications of life.*

Imagine the complications that will occur when a parent
knows a child is lying and protects the child by accepting
the child's lie. Consider the following example of a routine
middle school science project. The innocuous science project is a good barometer of parents' willingness to lie for
their children.

When my youngest son was in eighth grade, we attended the science fair with all the projects children allegedly built. I compelled my son to create his own project from basement items. His idea was not a technological wonder, but it was unique and it was his own creation. It was an obvious eighth-grade invention.

As we walked through the maze of science projects, I saw an incredible project that would have required a master's degree in engineering. As the boy's father, (who had a master's degree in engineering) explained how the project worked, his son appeared indifferent, even though he'd been awarded first prize. This father and son were presenting an obvious lie and they received an award for it.

Of course, there are more serious issues that parents can lie about for their children. The school board was about to kick a teenager off the team because he was caught drinking alcohol, which was against school policy. Although he was guilty, his mother lied for him. She told school officials that he was home the night he was accused of drinking. They accepted her lie and he stayed on the football team.

I later counseled the mother of the football player. She realized she had told a lie that had many consequences, including harm to her son's character, their relationship, and his view of the world. She had granted him permission to lie about any problems in life, with her as his accomplice.

Since she created a relationship with her son founded on distrust and dishonesty, she hindered her son's desire for truth and honesty. When distrust and dishonesty hold a relationship together, eventually the people involved have to ask themselves, "I wonder if he or she would lie to me too?"

Their relationship weakens when this thought surfaces, never allowing trust to grow.

Their shared lie will change her son's view of the world. Instead of viewing the world as a place to create trusting relationships, he may view the world as a chess game and view people as pawns that he can manipulate with dishonesty and deceit.

Too Trusting: Overindulgent parents are too trusting.

Some parents who have dishonest children are too gullible. Parents want to trust their children, but when children lie they are untrustworthy. Children who lie will often defend themselves by saying to their parents, "You should trust me!" This leads overindulgent parents to feel guilty for not trusting their children. They believe that if they were good parents, they would try to trust their children once again.

In counseling, many overindulgent parents say to me, "I know I should not have trusted my child, but I felt I should give my child one more chance." Because of this thought, their children continue to get "one more chance." Overindulgent parents are usually intelligent people who know they should not trust their children, but they ignore their good judgment.

A Mentoring Parent's Management of Children's Lying Behavior

Once you discover which of the overindulgent parenting principles you are using, replace these distorted thoughts by reviewing the qualities of the mentoring parent. Consider the following ideas and suggestions. Notice the suggestions that reflect the qualities of the mentoring parent will be in bold highlight.

- Mentoring parents have a **strong commitment to the truth.** It is important for children to learn that they cannot manipulate their parents with lies and deceit.

   When I was a child and in a little trouble, my father asked me 100 questions about the troubled situation. I answered every question, but I answered dishonestly— and was good at it. When he finished asking me questions, he seemed convinced that I was telling the truth. One week later, my father asked me the same one hundred questions. I struggled to recall all the original detailed lies that I said before, but I could not remember. My story was so inconsistent it was obvious that I was lying. My father thoughtfully said to me, "A liar always forgets." He also said to me, "You're a liar" and then he disciplined me. He instilled truth and honesty deep into my soul that day.

- There is no substitute for **truth and honesty.** There are no substitutes for truthful labels. When my father said, "You're a liar," I felt shame and humiliation. Shame and humiliation are natural emotions that can motivate positive change, when attached to good thinking. Because of this experience, my wanting to avoid shame and humiliation caused me to be honest. Honesty is a basic value that helps create good self-esteem, character, and relationships.

- When children exaggerate to get your attention, it is helpful to **consider the amount and quality of time you spend with your children.** Exaggeration suggests a child has unmet needs for attention. Be open to self-appraisal and to decide if you need to make changes with the time you spend with your children.

- To reduce gullibility and susceptibility to guilt trips, **trust your emotions and think more positively.** Indignation is an appropriate reaction when children try to manipulate with guilt. When children use guilt to manipulate you, your children are insulting you. They are suggesting that you are dumb enough to fall for their manipulative guilt trips. That is not the case, of course, but parents need to be aware of their children's shenanigans.

When Diana realized her daughter was trying to manipulate her, she became indignant, saying in a very rational tone, "You are trying to manipulate me with a guilt trip. It will not work. If you want something from me, you better be straightforward and honest. Then I will tell you how you can earn what you want. Guilt trips won't work."

Stealing

The Purpose of Stealing:

Young children occasionally take something that does not belong to them. Children may take a piece of candy from a grocery store, steal money from their parents, or heist a cherished toy from a sibling's bedroom. Most parents employ the traditional discipline of having their children apologize and make restitution.

As with persistent lying, persistent stealing in the form of shoplifting is both a serious psychological and legal issue. Manipulative lying usually accompanies children's stealing because they need to cover their tracks.

What is interesting about shoplifting is that most children who shoplift have money. They could easily buy the merchandise they are stealing. Most shoplifting children also know right from wrong. So why do children shoplift? Listed below are several common reasons:

1. The most common reason children shoplift is for a rush of excitement.

2. Some children shoplift to make their parents angry.

3. Other children shoplift to call attention to issues they find disturbing within their family.

4. Many children feel entitled and justified when stealing, because they believe they should be able to take whatever they want. These children have a greater commitment to stealing. They are usually candidates for the legal system because their stealing is persistent.

When caught, most children blame their friends for the shoplifting and claim they just happened to be there. This excuse is usually a premeditated lie. These children usually plan to steal. Parents need to hold shoplifting children accountable. If they don't, they may be using one of the following overindulgent parenting principles:

Indulgent Parenting Principles That Encourage Stealing:

> *Shield from Consequences: Overindulgent parents shield their children from the consequences of their children's actions as well as the complications of life.*

When parents pamper their children, their children expect special privileges. When police arrest an overindulged child, the child expects special privileges from the store owner and police. When the child does not receive special privileges from "others," he or she becomes angry at these authority figures.

Overindulged children who steal pick their own "point of responsibility." For example, when an overindulged boy misbehaves at school and is disciplined, he does not focus on the problem starting with his misbehavior. Instead, he picks another "point of responsibility." He proposes that the school officials are the problem, since they are overreacting. He believes the school officials are unfair because it is always someone else's fault.

Many shoplifting children do not believe the problem started with their decision to shoplift. The shoplifting child picks another "point of responsibility" and blames the store owner for being a jerk who has overreacted by calling the police. If the child's parents agree with the child, they will try to shield their child from appropriate consequences. This leads children to believe that others are unjustly punishing them, and consequently, they learn nothing about changing their behavior.

Overindulgent parents falsely inflate children's egos so children believe they are more capable than they are. Most children who shoplift believe they are much smarter than adults. They believe they can outsmart anyone, so when police arrest them, they are surprised.

A Mentoring Parent's Management of Children's Stealing Behavior:

One rule of thumb to offer parents is that once children steal, it is easier for them to steal again. Another rule of thumb states that if police arrest children for stealing, especially shoplifting, it is rarely their first theft.

Mentoring parents always have children confess, apologize, make restitution, and accept consequences when they steal. When children's stealing includes shoplifting, mentoring parents get counseling for their children. It is especially important that they also **do not buffer** their children from the legal **consequences** of shoplifting.

SUMMARY

Much of children's misbehavior is temporary. But misbehavior can become permanent and eventually damage parent-child relationships. We cannot always control our children's behavior. We do have control of how we choose to react to children when they misbehave. Always check your reactions to your children's misbehavior to determine if your reactions reflect any of the overindulgent parenting principles. Then correct your reactions by reviewing and incorporating the qualities of the mentoring parent.

In Chapter 5, you will receive many parenting tools that sharpen mentoring skills. Most overindulgent parents need these skills.

- CHAPTER 5 -

The "Tool Box" for the
Mentoring Parent

Changing from overindulgence to mentoring requires
specific parenting tools to build a better relationship with children. This chapter gives you the tools you
need to become mentoring parents. Use the tools you feel
most comfortable with, but also stretch and use tools that
may be new and unusual. Also, consider using a combination of these tools.

Children are so unique that one parenting tool may
work for one of your children, but the same tool may be
completely ineffective for other children. Mix these tools as
creatively as you can. It is also helpful to discuss and
rehearse these parenting ideas with each other.

Consider the parenting tools in this "Toolbox" designed
to give you the practical skills you need to become a mentoring parent.

Assessing Family Safety

It is vital for families to have a feeling of safety before
children are willing to make quality changes in their behav-

ior. Consider this question: "Does your family feel safe?" One way to assess the safe feeling within your family is to consider how you feel when you approach your home. Do you feel tension or apprehension? If not, great! If so, realize it is more difficult for children because they do not have the skills to manage tension.

Continually review and use the qualities of the mentoring parent. These qualities promote a safe and encouraging family atmosphere. You can further assess your family's safe feelings by considering the following questions:

- ◆ Is it safe and comfortable to discuss any issue in your family?
- ◆ Are you and your spouse united and bonded on most issues, especially in handling the children?
- ◆ Does your family routinely talk throughout the week?
- ◆ Is there a balance in your family relationships? In other words, is there one-on-one time with each child? Does the family do activities together? Are there spouse-only times?
- ◆ Do you give equal love to your children, but parent your children differently?

If you answer "yes" to most of these questions, then your family probably feels safe. If the answers are mostly "no," start using the qualities of the mentoring parent and the tools throughout this chapter.

Discipline by Design

Too often, discipline happens impulsively or not at all. Discipline needs planning and well-defined goals. Parents who plan discipline together have a greater bond and are more effective. Listed below is a good working foundation for discipline that I often suggest to parents.

1. When your children are misbehaving, forewarn them that discipline will occur if they continue.

2. It is helpful if you tell your children the exact misbehaviors they need to change before disciplining them. This alone may stop some of your children's misbehavior.

3. If the forewarning does not work, use discipline. I cannot advise you which discipline is the best all-purpose discipline. Each child is so unique that a discipline that is effective for one child may be ineffective for another child. My best suggestions are time-out, loss of special activities, temporary increase of chores, and extra homework.

4. After you discipline, tell your children exactly what they need to do differently and how they can make amends. Children need to change their misbehavior, but they also need a chance to redeem themselves, so offer exact instructions to your children on what they can do to make amends.

Consider the following example of a parent using a healthy foundation of discipline.

A dad instructed his ten-year-old son, who had terrible handwriting, to rewrite his homework. Although the boy promised his dad that he would do it, his father forewarned him that he would discipline him if he did not correct his homework. When the father came back several hours later to ask if the homework was complete, the boy assured him it was completed. When his father asked to see it, the boy hedged. It became obvious to the father that his son did not complete the homework. Finally the boy reluctantly offered his original work.

The father realized that he was looking at original homework. He told his son that he had committed two wrongs. First, he lied about his homework and lying was unacceptable behavior. Second, he did not rewrite his homework.

The father was consistent with his forewarning and disciplined the boy. After the discipline, the father clearly told the boy that he still needed to complete the work and to forget lying about it.

This boy felt guilty that he lied to his father, but his guilt is good guilt, because he was caught lying. Good guilt creates self-guidance that encourages children to correct their behavior in the future. This young man's self-guidance may say to him, "In order not to feel bad about lying, I need to do my work and tell the truth." He also felt disappointed in himself, but his disappointment passed. When he completed the work, he felt better. His father quickly approved his son's finished work.

This father had a firm parenting foundation that guided him. He did not grope for ideas on how to discipline his son. This parenting framework offered his son predictable guidance without a frustrated and ineffective parent. Also, this parent did not let his son off the hook. He taught him to be responsible.

Compare the above example with the example below of an ineffective discipline:

Before this same father incorporated this parenting foundation of the mentoring parent, he once had a bad day. His boy was reluctant to dress up to go to dinner at a fancy restaurant, and was raising a fuss.

"Okay, fine," said his frustrated father, "You can go to your grandmother's house while we go out to dinner." The father gave in to his son's demands and his boy was much happier.

On the way to his grandmother's house, his parents stopped to pick up the boy's favorite uncle, who was joining them for dinner. The boy had not realized his favorite uncle was going to dinner too. When they pulled their car into his grandmother's driveway, this boy refused to get out of the car because he wanted to go out to dinner with his favorite uncle. This father became frustrated, pulled the boy out of the car, spanked him hard, put him in his grandmother's house and left, never saying one word.

In this case, this boy did not feel good guilt that could guide his behavior. He felt intense anger. His father offered no quality communication, before or after the discipline. Instead, his father reacted with frustration and created an angry son who felt no compunction to correct his behavior. His son felt justified in his anger.

If parents offer their children a parenting foundation (such as the discipline guidelines mentioned above), parents can instill a different attitude and motivation in their children.

Forewarning

Forewarning, briefly mentioned above, is such an important parenting technique it needs more discussion. Very few overindulgent parents forewarn and follow through. Calmly and firmly offer forewarnings. It is important that you give only one forewarning, because it is easy for overindulgent parents to give too many forewarnings and reduce its effectiveness. By the way, children do not usually show that they appreciate a forewarning, but they do.

Another important reason to forewarn children is that as parents manage their children's behavior, this management creates emotions within their children. As a metaphor, think about your emotional reaction when a police officer stops you for speeding, but gives you a warning. When a police officer gives you this "forewarning," you have a good feeling about this police officer. If another police officer stops you, you know you will probably get a ticket. Whether you like to admit it or not, getting that ticket makes sense because you were forewarned. Whether children admit it or not, they will feel that their parent's forewarned discipline makes sense, too.

Paying Money for Discipline

When my children were small (four and five years old), they enjoyed sharing the same bedroom together. There are many advantages to young children having the same bedroom, but there is also one major disadvantage. They have difficulty falling asleep. In fact, they get rowdy.

I found this frustrating as I sat in the living room and listened to their thumping footsteps upstairs, well past their bedtime. Discipline did not help. They just kept thumping.

An idea popped into my head. I went shopping and bought them wallets. They were ecstatic with their new wallets; all made with neat leather and super-hero emblems. I told them I was going to give them an allowance and they hit the ceiling with happiness.

They had a wallet and they had money—$2 every week.

At bedtime that evening, I could hear their usual thumping. When I went upstairs, I forewarned them: "When Dad is at work, he helps fix children's behavior and they pay him for this help. So, every time I come up here and tell you to stay in bed and go to sleep, you will each have to pay me $1."

They were standing on their beds and looked at each other and blinked. They looked at me with an expression resembling, "Yeah, right!" I went downstairs and in less than two minutes I heard that familiar thumping noise. I went upstairs and said, "I am here to fix your behavior by telling you to go to bed. That will be one dollar." They went to their wallets and each gave me one dollar. I eventually earned enough money to buy lunch and I never heard any thumping noise again.

Younger children respond well to this technique. It is so important that children work to earn their allowance. Unfortunately, this is not happening in most families today. Many parents are being "five-dollared" into financial straits by children calling parents cheap as they complain, "It's only five dollars!" Children need to earn their money and they need to pay for their disciplines. When they do not earn their money, they will ask for money and do nothing to earn it. Imagine asking your boss for extra money and offering nothing in return. The world does not work that way and neither should parenting.

A "Problem-Solving" Attitude

When something goes wrong in life, a healthy question for parents to ask is, "What are my choices to correct this situation?" This is the cornerstone of success in life, and especially for successful parenting. Children need to see their parents' problem-solving attitude, especially when they are on the receiving end of advice or discipline.

Children gain this problem-solving attitude when parents guide and discipline them. Consider the common example of a child with a bully bothering him:

Problem-Solving Issue # 1: Parents can help a child gather all the relevant facts. Where does this occur? Who knows about it? What does the bully want?

Problem-Solving # 2: Parents can offer insights by explaining why someone chooses to be a bully. They can tell children that bullies need to feel "bully power" because they do not have real empowerment in their life.

Problem-Solving # 3: Parents can help their child assess all the possible choices. If the bully hangs out in one area, the child could stay away from that area, tell a teacher. or try to stay with a group.

Problem-Solving # 4: Then parents allow their child to pick one of the choices. It is tempting for parents to lead a child toward a particular choice, but it is important the child make the choice. Making choices is an important life-sustaining skill.

Problem-Solving # 5: Parents can allow the child to live with the decision for some time, then help the child to evaluate if the choice is working. Does it need changing? Does a different choice need consideration?

As you teach this "problem-solving" framework to your children, youngsters can eventually use these skills when you are not around. This helps children gain self-guidance, self-reliance and self-confidence.

Self Appraisal

Many parents do a wonderful job encouraging and praising their children. Encouragement involves positive statements parents use to keep children motivated toward self-improvement. Praise is the tribute children receive once they arrive at a behavior change. Mentoring parents praise children with love, affection, and status. They do not give toys and activities since their praise is a bond with their children.

Another helpful tool parents can give their children to increase self-reliance and self-esteem is self-appraisal. For example:

> *Ted came home with a good report card and gave it to his mother. Mom, who encourages Ted with his studies, exclaims, "That's great!" (Praise). To create self-appraisal and increase self-reliance, Ted's mom may ask, "How do you feel about your grades?" This helps Ted create an independent self-appraisal.*

Sometimes self-appraisal feels bad because children have negative qualities or experience failure. To train children to cope with these difficult times without self-criticism is a critical balance for parents to achieve. In gradual steps, encourage your children with honest appraisals of their progress. By asking them how they feel about their progress, you are helping your children feel the emotional change that comes with the behavioral change.

For example, a good boss can correct an employee with care and sincerity, while pointing-out flaws that need correction. As the corrections occur, the good boss continues to praise the employee, and the employee feels better. A lousy boss condemns and criticizes an employee, which increases the employee's anger, frustration, and opposition. By offering care, sincerity, encouragement, praise, and honest appraisal to their children, parents can guide them to appraise their own progress.

Not-So-Natural Consequences

There has been notable discussion in this book about allowing children to endure the natural consequences of their misbehavior. Natural consequences are consequences that occur naturally in a situation. For example, if a girl does not study for a test, she may fail. If a teenage boy does not maintain his car, the car naturally falls apart. These are natural consequences. On the other hand, "not-so-natural" consequences can be by parental design. "Not-so-natural" consequences have a great advantage over natural consequences because parents can safely use them without the damaging effects of natural consequences. For example:

Nancy habitually parked her car in the street on snowy nights. Her parents forewarned her the city may tow her car away if the snowplows came through during the night. I suggested to her parents a "not-so-natural" consequence.

Instead of allowing the natural consequences of the city towing her car away when she did not move the car, her parents parked her car in their garage. In the morning, Nancy was worried because her car was gone, until her parents told her it was in the garage.

She experienced the emotion of her car being towed, without having to experience the actual event. You would think Nancy had learned a valuable lesson.

Believe it or not, it did not help. The next snowy evening, Nancy left her car parked in the street again. In spite of her parents' insistence, she left it there. That night, her parents put her car in the garage to prevent the city from towing her car away. The next morning when she saw her car was not in the street, she went directly to the garage to get her car, but she could not find her keys. Her mother told Nancy that to get her keys, she would have to pay her parents a $35 towing fee.

The next snowy night, Nancy parked her car in the driveway. Nancy's parents offered Nancy "not-so-natural" consequences which allowed her to experience the consequence of losing her car and paying a fee.

Notice the learning experience was not effective until Nancy paid a $35 fine to her parents. It is very helpful to blend various parenting tools together. Nancy's discipline included "not-so-natural consequences" and paying for her lack of discipline.

"Not-so-natural consequences" is one of my favorite parenting tools, because you can become very creative with this tool. Here are several more examples where this parenting tool has a good impact:

Glenda is fifteen-years-old and shares a bathroom with her parents. Every morning when her dad gets into the bathroom, Glenda's makeup, hair dryer, curling iron, deodorant, and shampoo are disarrayed throughout the bathroom. Nothing is in its place!

I advised her dad to forewarn his daughter once that he would confiscate her bathroom "stuff" the next time it was left out, and she would not get it back. She tested his warning and lost all of her grooming paraphernalia, because I advised her dad to throw out her stuff. When she failed to keep her things in order, her stuff was gone—history! The result is a fifteen-year-old girl facing school without her make-up, cologne, deodorant, hair spray, and shampoo. It was important that her dad's confiscation be consistent, and that she replace her supplies with her own money. Eventually, Glenda realized that to keep her "stuff," she needed to put it away.

Since clothes and toys are too expensive to throw away, I advise parents to lock them up when using the confiscation technique. Parents can gradually give clothes and toys back, as their children's cleanliness improves.

Another example involves Alex, a bright boy who refused to work hard in school and had the uncanny ability to make his homework his parents' problem. Although he never worried about his near-failing grades, his parents did. Despite their best efforts, Alex refused to do the homework.

Often when I have counseled on this issue, I suggest a two-step technique.

***Step 1:** I recommend that parents forewarn children about natural consequences. For example, when an intellectually bright child like Alex refuses to work and his parents offer every form of help, I forewarn him about the future. "When you are 18 and graduating (we hope) from high school, your parents will be* *free to do whatever they want. They'll have more money, might retire, who knows." This leaves the impression that Alex's grades will have no affect on the quality of his parents' lives. I continue, "At age 18, what you did or did not do in high school is your problem. You will have to explain to a potential employer why you have a 1.4 grade point average." Alex said, "I don't care," but he still got the message.*

Step 2: *I also tell parents this problem is an ownership issue. Is it their problem or Alex's problem? Next, I advised Alex's parents to do something that is difficult for invested parents to do: to let go of ownership of Alex's education. No more nagging about homework or assignments. No pressure to achieve. I told his parents that this problem belongs to Alex. When his parents gave up ownership, Alex had to decide if he would accept ownership of his schoolwork or not. He lost the power of pushing his parents' educational button in order to frustrate and worry them. I directed Alex's parents to focus on retirement plans. I suggested they could use his college fund for retirement. Studying is now Alex's problem. Going to college is now Alex's problem.*

Many children intentionally get low grades to push their parents' buttons. The above two-step strategy erases parents' reactions when their educational buttons are pushed. Often parents find themselves in a never-ending cycle of their children's sabotage. Since parents are continuously telling their children how important grades are, their children use this information to anger their parents. The more parents try, the less these children work.

Instead, parents can use the two-step process of forewarning, and give back ownership (and all its consequences) to the underachieving child. I understand this is difficult for parents. I remind parents that many people who were successful in life performed poorly in high school.

If parents offer the idea that life is over because of their children's poor high school performance, children grow up believing it. Everyone grows at different rates physically, academically, emotionally, cognitively, socially, and spiritually. I tell parents to remember their high school reunion and consider the people they never expected to do well, but did.

As an aside, I do not believe in paying for children's college. College offers two types of education: a special field of study that students are interested in pursuing, and a money management degree. As college students pay for their own college, they learn resourcefulness when times are tight, as well as decision-making related to cash flow and spending. Overindulged children do not gain this second education, which is as important as a field of study. College students have many choices in paying for their college today. Ask any college guidance counselor if you want more information. Better yet, have your college-bound child make the inquiry.

Get rid of the fear that poor high school achievement will damage your children's future. When children decide it is time to succeed, they will. Like everyone else, they will have to pay their dues. That is a natural consequence.

Refinement

Think back to the previous example of Nancy's car being towed. It illustrates another parenting tool Nancy's parents used—refinement. The first time Nancy's parents put her car in the garage, their strategy did not work. Nancy still parked her car on the street during snowy nights. Her parents did not give up. Instead, they refined their discipline by adding another tool (making Nancy pay for her discipline).

One of the greatest parenting flaws I have witnessed is that many parents try a new parenting tool once and then give up in frustration because the tool did not work. Some parents will say, "We have tried everything and nothing works with this child." On a rare occasion, this may be true. What I usually see is parents drifting from one parenting tool to another without refining their parenting tools.

Refinement is essential for parenting, especially for parents of young children because they are more likely to model their parents. If their parents are adapting by refining their parenting tools, children also will learn to adapt and to refine.

There are several ways to refine discipline. They include:

1. Realize the same discipline may not work for all children, because of the unique features of different children.

2. Try blending a combination of several parenting tools to create more effective discipline.

3. Don't believe it when your children seem unaffected by discipline! Children often pretend discipline does not bother them. Continue to be persistent with your planned discipline, and consider yourself successful by keeping your parenting plan in place. When children pretend a discipline does not bother them, parents often give up on a discipline, which reinforces the child's disobedience. Be persistent with your parenting plan! Remember, you can only control your actions, not your children's reactions.

Classify Behavior

To help decide the severity of children's misbehavior, it is helpful to learn to classify children's behavior:

- *Good behavior* leads children to receive rewards and creates positive self-guidance.
- A *behavioral concern* is a misbehavior that is not particularly harmful to the child or others.
- An *alarming behavior* is children's misbehavior that has the potential to be emotionally or physically hurtful to someone. An "alarming behavior" is noticeable and persistent. Parents need a parenting plan to help their children remove alarming behavior.
- An *extreme behavior* is a child's misbehavior that is hurting someone and needs immediate attention, a parenting plan, and possibly counseling. A pattern of extreme behavior suggests conduct disorder.

These classifications are helpful to determine if you should simply ignore your children's misbehavior, institute a parenting plan based on the principles of this book, or initiate counseling.

Discipline Without an Audience

The goal of discipline does not include embarrassment or humiliation of children. On the contrary, it means teaching children to learn, bond, and experience the consequences of making decisions, both good and bad. It is not always possible, but usually best if you discipline children in private. This lessens their embarrassment and humiliation.

180

There are two notable exceptions to this rule:

1. There are times when it may be necessary to discipline children in front of their friends, especially if the misbehavior is extreme and harmful. The priority of removing the potential harm to others may override the concern for the child's personal embarrassment.

2. Some children have poor self-guidance because their overindulgent parents protected them from natural embarrassment and humiliation. They have never learned the impact of their behavior on others. Public discipline that includes feedback from children they hurt may help them understand their impact on others.

Children, like adults, need to be humbled, but excessive and distorted embarrassment and humiliation can erode self-esteem. Usually, discipline offered privately is best. Again, there would need to be special circumstances to discipline children in front of others as mentioned above. As a parent, I have used discipline in front of others and learned it is best to offer a forewarning first. If parents forewarn children first, then discipline their children in public if the misbehavior continues, the next time parents forewarn their children, they are usually more responsive.

Ignoring Children's Behavior

Ignoring children's behavior is a highly overrated parenting tool. It can be appropriate with minor misbehavior in young children, if their behavior is annoying and attention-getting. Often children are getting too much attention from other children when they misbehave, so this tool becomes ineffective.

Coaching, Rehearsal, and Choices

I am going to tell you a secret that I never share with any children, but will share with you. When it comes to their children, parents have no power! Parents have power when their children are young, but power fades fast as children become teenagers.

Teenagers need their parents' influence. That is why your sound advice and predictions for your children are so important. When your children have confidence in the consistency of your advice and predictions, you gain more influence as your children mature.

Coach, rehearse, and give children the gradual power to make their own choices. This is incredibly important because today's children have many sources for bad advice and more disturbing models for misbehavior than ever before. In other words, today's parents have more competition than ever before—competition that influences children's beliefs, and competition which often runs counter to parent's beliefs. An excellent strategy is to combine coaching, rehearsal, and choice.

Coaching:

Coaching occurs when you give children good instructions and predictions. It is vital that your style of coaching needs to change as your children become teenagers and adults. For purposes of safety, parents need to be over-controlling when their children are toddlers because of their inability to understand what may harm them. For example, toddlers do not realize that a wall socket could shock them. So, parents need to over-control their children until they are old enough to realize the dangerous issues of life.

For the first several years, parents' over-control of their children protects their children. As children grow, parents need to change. The goal for parents, as children turn into adults, is to be less controlling and to become more influential. You can accomplish this by using the qualities of the mentoring parent and the parenting tools provided in this chapter.

Each child grows at a different rate, so it is difficult to tell you exactly when you need to become more "influential" and less "controlling." Some parents never make the transition from control talk to coaching. We discussed an example earlier where I counseled one mother who talked to her married daughter as if her daughter was a toddler. This mother was demanding. She used her money to make her daughter bend to her wishes because her daughter was financially dependent.

She was controlling many parts of her daughter's marital relationship and childrearing. When I counseled her about her need to control her daughter, she realized she never made the transition from control talk to coaching. She also realized that she never created her own identity. She was trying to live her life through her daughter.

Rehearsal:

Children benefit from rehearsal since rehearsal is one of the best methods for changing behavior. Parents often tell children what not to do when they misbehave. When parents tell their children how to improve their behavior, they may not fully understand. As you know, children's brains do not perform like adult brains!

When adults receive verbal instruction, they have abstract reasoning, so they can easily imagine the actual changes they need to make. Children on the other hand have a harder time imagining these changes. It is helpful if they actually experience them.

With rehearsal, you can help your children physically practice the exact behaviors they need to use. Your children can experiment with various behaviors to help decide which options are best. Rehearsal allows children to be comfortable with new choices before they actually try them at home, in school, and on the playground.

Rehearsal is natural for children because it is exactly like something with which they are familiar—childhood play. For example, parents of the 1950s were used to screen doors that closed with a spring. These doors would bang loudly when children let go of them. For some reason, slamming doors irritated 1950s parents. They did not say, "Don't slam the door!" Instead, they instructed their children to go outside and walk through the door again, without slamming the door. Teachers use rehearsal all day with children. When children run in a hallway, teachers ask the "sprinters" to back up and walk the entire distance again. This is how rehearsal works.

Use rehearsal for all types of behavior problems. It is especially helpful when children are in difficult situations and you cannot be there to help. For example:

Eight-year-old Jackie's uncle would often ask her gossip-type questions when she visited his home. He would isolate her and interrogate her. She felt trapped and uncomfortable because he was so big and she was so small.

Just before their next visit to her uncle's home, Jackie discussed this problem with her mother and me. I suggested that we rehearse several scenarios for her to use when her uncle asked his meddlesome questions.

On her next visit, her uncle employed his usual tactics, and started to ask intrusive gossip-type ques-

tions about her family. Jackie took her uncle by the hand and said, "Come with me." He followed her into the living room, where her parents were sitting. Just like she'd rehearsed she announced, "He is asking me all those stupid questions again." Then she looked at him and said, "You can ask my parents those same questions."

Her rehearsed solution was empowering. It helped her gain the support of her parents and the freedom to play with her cousins—without her uncle's harassment. Another easy solution would have been to have one of her parents talk to the uncle. But that solution would not have offered several important lessons:

- Jackie learned that her mentoring parents could offer real solutions, so when difficult times occur, Jackie will more than likely go to her parents for guidance.

- Jackie realized that her parents can help her feel empowered. This is vital in parenting! If she knows she can go to her mentoring parents for real solutions, she feels more protected.

- Jackie has a new skill, the power of rehearsal. When she rehearses other issues, she can plan her actions before she proceeds. When young children rehearse solutions with their parents, they become older children who can mentally rehearse choices before taking an action.

A group of boys taunted 15-year-old Randy by continually following him and threatening to beat him up. His parents tried everything to stop this taunting from escalating into a major conflict. Because these

bullying boys had only threatened, no authority could take action and their uninvolved parents offered no help.

Randy's parents advised him to always contact the police when the boys threatened him. When the youngster asked a police officer about this problem, the officer discouraged him from fighting since it was illegal. But the officer gave him an idea. He told Randy that in a group of bullies, the bully in the group with the biggest mouth was often the bully with the smallest body. The police officer suggested that if they isolate Randy, he should challenge the smallest of the group to fight one-on-one. Randy's father rehearsed this idea with Randy.

The police officer was right. The smallest boy in the group did have the biggest mouth. One day they ambushed Randy in an alley, but as they pushed him around, he challenged the smallest instigator. The entire group watched the little instigator, who began to sweat. Finally, the instigator backed down and this group did not bother Randy again.

This is a tough and risky tactic. As a psychologist, I usually do not advise children to fight. But events in life force children into difficult situations, which require difficult decisions. Not fighting is a principle many parents teach their children, but should boys like Randy allow five teenagers to beat them up and do nothing? We taught Randy that fighting is a last resort and, if possible, he should avoid fighting. It is a risky strategy, but it worked in Randy's case. Mentoring parents teach their children the rules of life. But, they also teach children the exceptions to the rules.

Rehearsal empowers children. It also bonds children with their mentoring parents. Rehearsing choices with children gives them the opportunity to practice and gain more tools to manage difficult situations.

There are times when you cannot directly help your children correct a problem. But you can design opportunities for your children to rehearse sticky situations. To cite a specific example:

Mitch's father saw few social skills in his 14-year-old son. His son was lonely, and ate lunch every day in the school cafeteria by himself. In fact, he did everything alone. The father did not know how to teach his son to socialize with other children, so he contacted a network of trained students and counselors who helped children with various problems. The coordinating school counselor of the school's peer program was glad to help.

When Mitch went to the cafeteria to eat alone, a student sat in front of him and casually talked with him. Then another student sat next to him and talked to him too. He got his first invitation to a football game. Several months later, the school peer program invited him to join. He became a peer counselor.

This mentoring father realized that if children interacted with his son, his son could model their social skills. All he had to do was discover how to expose his son to social children. Because he found a way to make this happen, Mitch never ate alone again and he developed many friendships. That's a mentoring parent!

Choice:

The more choices children have for solutions, the better. I usually like to rehearse more than one choice when children have any problem, so they have many possible solutions. Even nonassertive children make at least one attempt to change a problem into a solution. If one choice does not work, the children are encouraged to try the next choice.

Rules About Rules

There are "rules about rules" that our children need to learn. For example, mentoring parents advocate that children should not fight, but they do not want their children beaten without defending themselves. The rule is "do not fight," but children need to know the exceptions to the rules.

This is often a problem for children when there are situations with conflicting values. They are uncertain which values they should prioritize. For example, if a child sees a friend do something illegal, such as steal from a store, the child may have difficulty deciding which value has a greater priority. Should loyalty to a friend take precedence over not keeping secrets from parents? Mentoring parents can prepare children by discussing examples of these moral dilemmas long before these moral crises occur. Parents must teach their children the "rules about rules."

In the example of loyalty to friends versus keeping secrets from parents, the "rules about rules" dilemma depends on which value has a greater priority for the parents. If parents believe that loyalty to friends is the most important priority, then parents would teach their children when loyalty to friends becomes illegal behavior. If parents believe the most important priority is not keeping secrets from parents, then parents would teach their children how to keep confidentiality, and how to make appropriate exceptions.

Unfortunately, teaching children "rules about rules" rarely happens until a problem occurs, when knowing the "rules about rules" would have been helpful. Mentoring parents can rehearse with their children the "rules about rules" philosophy and offer children possible solutions for future moral dilemmas.

Rehearsal is a good technique, but there is no guarantee that children will choose rehearsed solutions. Even though children may not use the rehearsed solutions when a moral problem occurs, they eventually realize the rehearsed solutions would have produced a better outcome. This realization will help shape their decisions in the future.

Compliment Good Behavior

Complimenting good behavior is a technique that works well for younger children, especially with their shorter attention span. Kindergarten teachers are experts with this tool. For example, when kindergarten teachers mention that one child is behaving well, the other children start behaving with the hope of getting their teacher's compliment.

Younger children automatically respect their teacher, but this is not usually true of some older children. If a high school teacher compliments one student's behavior during class, other students often ridicule the complimented child.

However, children of all ages need compliments. With younger children, parents can give compliments to change children's behavior. With older children, parents should give compliments without attempting to change their behavior. Older children need honest compliments that offer encouragement.

I tell parents of younger children to use compliments to encourage their children and to change children's behavior. I encourage parents of older children to eliminate hidden agendas when using compliments, and praise them purely for the sake of complimenting.

"Thinking–Feeling" Questions and Making Amends

One mentoring tool that increases parents' influence to help their children understand their impact on others is to ask children "thinking and feeling" questions. For example:

"How do you think Grandmother felt when you gave her flowers?"

"What do you think it feels like to be punched the way you punched your brother?"

"How did you feel when you gave money to that charity?"

"How would you feel if someone stole your favorite toy?"

Mentoring parents ask children "thinking-feeling" questions to motivate them to think about how they effect others. One mother saw her son intentionally break his friend's favorite toy. This mentoring mother asked her son a "thinking-feeling" question so he would understand how his actions affected his friend. To make amends, she also instructed him to give his favorite toy to his friend.

"Thinking and feeling" questions teach children to think twice before they act, and promote empathy for others. Through "thinking and feeling" questions, children learn that making amends heals relationships and helps them realize that we are all connected and interdependent.

Align Children's Feelings and Thoughts

Because children are beginning to learn about their emotions, they often confuse emotional words. When a boy says, "I hate my sister!" parents often respond, "No, you don't!" But for that moment, this boy is actually angry with his sister. In another instant, the children are often playing together. Children have difficulty distinguishing between different emotions. When this boy is calmer, he needs to be mentored to use correct words such as, "I am angry with my sister."

When teaching children about the abstract words of emotions, I have found that a children's dictionary is helpful because it gives parents a simple way to express abstract words to children. Teach your children the accurate meaning for the words of emotions.

Eliminate Judgmental Talk

Have you ever screamed at any of your children, "What is wrong with you?" This is a tough question for children to hear. Their answers to this question can be even tougher. This question, "What is wrong with you?" is actually a broad-brush statement which leads children to believe they have flaws of which they are unaware.

Judgmentalness occurs when parents distort their children's understanding of themselves. Judgmental talk requires the use of distorted labels. When children are described as bad, they may accept this distorted label. Since judgmental talk is distorting children's view of themselves, parents need to remove distorted judgmental talk.

Judgmental talk does not include conversations when parents are honestly pointing out children's flaws. It is a mentoring parents job to point out and help correct children's flaws, and at the same time assure children that they can change.

Personal Empowerment

Children need to learn what they can influence and what they cannot influence. This is an idea that mentoring parents need to teach their children. For example, if there is a death, divorce, or other trauma, parents can teach their children what they can and cannot change about the difficult life experience.

I counsel many children who fantasize that if they are good, keep their grades up, help more around the house, then their parents will not divorce or their dead loved one will come back. While it is important for children and parents to express all of their emotions about a traumatic event, we must empower traumatized children with the truth, using as much diplomacy and empathy as the situation allows.

Touching Messages of Love

Frequent hugs and caring touch are important for growing children. Parents can create a bond by gently touching a child's shoulder. Most children are comfortable with different forms of physical affection. Mentoring parents can gauge the type of affection with which each of their children is comfortable, and use it.

Younger children may be more comfortable with a big burley hug, while teenagers seem to be uncomfortable with physical affection from their parents. Parents may need to get creative to keep physical affection alive with their teenagers.

One form of affectionate touch that most mothers hate is wrestling. I am convinced that father and son wrestling is the teenage form of hugging, but I am having a hard time convincing mothers of this fact! Mothers are typically upset with wrestling dads and teenagers in the living room, but it is a great way for self-conscious teenagers to preserve a touching relationship.

Some children are open to physical affection when their friends are not around. Other children are responsive to a touch on the shoulder or back, while others feel comfortable with a full bear hug. The important point is that you need to preserve physical affection with your children.

Humor

More than any other parenting tool, I have ended many heated family battles with humor. Here are several rules for using humor:

1. Humor should not hurt or put-down others.
2. Humor should not avoid or make light of important issues.
3. Humor should be directed at the situation and not at family members involved in a conflict.
4. Humor should not be overused.
5. Humor is a tool that is acceptable for parents to use with all types of children's misbehavior, except "extreme behavior" that is harmful to others.

When family tension needs decompression, humor and rage are two tools for releasing that tension. I prefer humor, since it is less abusive than rage. Humor can also strengthen the bond between parents and children that rage can never offer.

*One of my favorite examples of humor occurred
when a girl tried to push her mother's button to make
her angry. Instead of reacting with her predictable
temper tantrum, her mother started singing, "The
hills are alive with the sound of music..." As she
danced through the house the entire family started to
sing, leaving her daughter both shocked and perplexed! Her mother was humorously saying, "You will
not push my buttons." Instead of angrily confronting her
daughter, she turned it into a positive experience.*

Humor can create wonderful memories that last a lifetime,
and it is much more effective than intimidation and rage
because it promotes a safe and harmonious family atmosphere.

Humility

"When I'm wrong, I'm wrong." Parents admitting
when they are wrong sounds obvious, but the number of
families I have counseled where parents never admit it when
they are wrong is astounding. Often these same parents
become upset when their children never admit when they
are wrong. They wonder, "Where did this child learn to be
so stubborn?"

Admitting their mistakes and making apologies keep
people humble and willing to accept their own flaws, which
is the first step in correcting flaws.

In fact, if parents model humility, they will create humble and respectful children. When parents refuse to admit to
mistakes, their children assume that it is not safe to apologize or make amends. Admitting their mistakes and offering
apologies are good tools for building children's character.
Humility is an excellent quality for parents to model for
their children.

Time-Out

The first time I used time-out, I got the strongest arm muscles I have ever had. I decided that I was going to use a comfortable chair in my bedroom as the time-out chair for my children. It was a boring place with no toys, distractions, or entertainment.

When my youngest son was three, he was "strong-willed," so I created a parenting plan using time-out. When he misbehaved, I placed him in the time-out chair while I calmly explained the behaviors he needed to change. As I left, he followed me out the door and down the hall. During the next hour, I placed him back into that time-out chair over 100 times. He was testing me to the point of fatigue! If I had given up, his misbehavior would have continued. I was so persistent that I got a great set of arm muscles by constantly lifting him back into the chair. Finally, he stayed in the time-out chair. Eventually, this bedroom chair became his place to "cool off." He would often go in there on his own accord when he felt tempted to misbehave.

He would often stay there 30-to-45 minutes and leave with a positive attitude. Instead of the time-out chair becoming a notorious punishment, it became a tool to help him release pressure. Recently we tried to throw this old chair out, but he wanted us to keep it because it was his childhood "cooling off" chair. It sits in his room today and I suspect now that he is an adult, he will take it with him when he leaves.

Time-out has real advantages because it is neither an intrusive nor a physically painful discipline. Time-out allows time for children to think and cool off—or fall asleep. Parents also get a break (when the testing is over) when they use time-out. Time-out's greatest advantage is its potential in becoming a "cooling off" catalyst.

Spanking

I advise parents to not spank—but then there are "rules about rules." Is there ever a time when spanking is acceptable and not damaging to children?

Some parents should never spank their children. This is especially true of abusive parents. For other children, it is an individual decision for parents. Like most issues in life, there are no black and white answers. Most people who say they will never spank children either do not have children, have young children, or they allow their children to become unruly.

I do not agree with the current trend of psychological thought that says all spanking is bad and that it is always damaging to children. I do agree that spanking needs to be part of a parenting plan which stops spanking from becoming abusive. Here are my suggestions, if parents feel that spanking is suitable for their children:

1. Spanking is appropriate for strong-willed children who do not respond to other forms of discipline.

2. Spanking should be a final resort, after all other types of discipline have failed.

3. Parents should never spank children when they feel overwhelming frustration.

4. If one parent is not comfortable with spanking, the other parent needs to respect that discomfort and not

spank their children. Like any other discipline, parents need to agree before using the discipline of spanking.

5. Parents should always forewarn children before spanking them.

6. Parents need to state the exact misbehavior children need to change.

7. After the spanking, parents need to teach their children about the amends children need to do to correct their misbehavior.

8. Parents should offer a mild-to-moderate spanking on children's buttocks and never slap children on the face or head.

Spanking should not be a daily event. If it is, parents need to consider other kinds of discipline or family counseling.

SUMMARY

Mentoring parents use a creative combination of parenting tools when raising their children. They realize that although one parenting tool is not effective for some children, the same parenting tool can be effective for other children. Mentoring parents constantly refine and adjust their parenting plans. They always try to discover the best combination of parenting tools for their children.

When you have special parenting concerns, review the qualities of the mentoring parents, as well as the helpful tools of this chapter.

- Final Thoughts -

There are different challenges in parenting today that never existed before. In the 1940s, parents saw their children leave for a devastating war. In the 1960s, parents saw their children go to Vietnam or "trip out" on heavy drug involvement.

Today the challenges are different, but just as difficult. Today's parents have more competition influencing their children than ever before. The number one culprit influencing children is the media, which bombards our children with anti-adult messages, self-centeredness, and materialism. Watch Nickelodeon in the afternoon and you can see a stupid camp counselor, dumb teachers, bungling school principals, and idiotic parents.

There are countless reasons parents are losing their influence with children: lack of government support for families, rising divorce rates, loss of an active religious life, mobility, and more. Parents need a system that increases their influence with their children.

It is my hope that this book is part of the solution for you. Overindulgence is a major challenge for most well-intentioned parents.

This book has described how children feel entitled and angry when they are overindulged. Their feelings of entitlement and anger are affecting schools and communities. More importantly, families are not experiencing the rich and deep bonds of love, joy, safety, and security they need to build solid family relationships.

I mentioned hope in the beginning of this book. Hope is the wish for change, but taking action is the agent of change. I hope this book is an agent of change for you and your family—and I hope and pray you can create the close emotional bonds that you desire and deserve.

Index

Index

ASPE Cares About You and Your Children

As the exclusive distributor of this book and associated Overindulged Children™ products and services, ASPE is passionate about serving parents and young people with what Dr. Fogarty affectionately calls "good thinking."

The Overindulged Children™ professional seminar has swept the country, making it abundantly clear that parents and professionals are frustrated because they don't have the tools they need to counter the overwhelming effects of overindulgence. Parents, psychologists, educators, counselors, therapists and social workers have flooded our phones with questions. Professionals are looking for proven ways to help families. Quite often parents exhibit desperation or a silent resignation in their calls.

With this book, Dr. Fogarty helps you sort through the reasons you do the things you do and the effects they have on your children. He's seen it in years and years of counseling, teaching and training—and he wants you to take advantage of what he's learned as a parent and a psychologist.

Dr. Fogarty believes passionately that overindulgence is preventing many young people from developing healthy relationships and living responsible, happy lives. At ASPE, we agree. That's why together Dr. Fogarty and ASPE have created a suite of products that will help you mentor your child in specific behavioral principles.

We invite you to revisit this book often to find the tidbits of information that will help you and your children. Access our website at **www.aspeonline.com/parentbook** for even more great information that supports parents, children, families and the professionals who care for them.

Conrad Stuntz   Toll-free 877-800-5221
ASPE • 1400 Crescent Green, Suite 230• Cary, NC 27511